D0455435

# AN AUDIENCE OF ONE

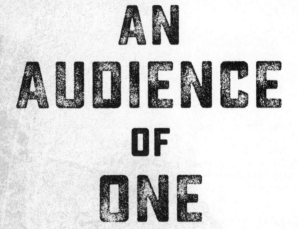

# AN
# AUDIENCE
## OF
## ONE

### Reclaiming Creativity
### for Its Own Sake

## SRINIVAS RAO
### WITH ROBIN DELLABOUGH

PORTFOLIO / PENGUIN

Portfolio/Penguin
An imprint of Penguin Random House LLC
375 Hudson Street
New York, New York 10014

Most Portfolio books are available at a discount when purchased in quantity for sales promotions or corporate use. Special editions, which include personalized covers, excerpts, and corporate imprints, can be created when purchased in large quantities. For more information, please call (212) 572-2232 or email specialmarkets@penguinrandomhouse .com. Your local bookstore can also assist with discounted bulk purchases using the Penguin Random House corporate Business-to-Business program. For assistance in locating a participating retailer, email B2B@penguinrandomhouse.com.

Library of Congress Cataloging-in-Publication Data

Names: Rao, Srinivas (Host of *The Unmistakable Creative* podcast), author. |
    Dellabough, Robin, author.
Title: An Audience of One: Reclaiming Creativity for Its Own Sake /
    Srinivas Rao with Robin Dellabough.
Description: New York: Portfolio/Penguin, [2018] | Includes bibliographical references
    and index.
Identifiers: LCCN 2018005892 (print) | LCCN 2018013640 (ebook) |
    ISBN 9781101981757 (ePub) | ISBN 9781101981733 (hardcover)
Subjects: LCSH: Creative ability in business. | Creative ability. | Success. |
    Success in business.
Classification: LCC HD53 (ebook) | LCC HD53 .R353 2018 (print) | DDC 650.1—dc23
LC record available at https://lccn.loc.gov/2018005892

Printed in the United States of America
10  9  8  7  6  5  4  3  2  1

Book design by Kristin del Rosario

*To my father,*
*who instilled in me a lifelong love of music*
*and taught me to appreciate the beauty*
*that emerges when we truly listen;*
*and to my mother,*
*who instilled in me a love of books.*

# CONTENTS

INTRODUCTION 1

PART ONE
Listening to Creativity 17

PART TWO
Listening to Yourself 35

PART THREE
Listening to Your Environment 79

PART FOUR
Listening to Others 149

PART FIVE
Not a Conclusion 191

Acknowledgments 199
Resources 201
Index 205

# AN AUDIENCE OF ONE

# INTRODUCTION

avid Bowie was arguably one of the greatest creatives of the last fifty years. By the time he died in 2016, he had produced no fewer than thirty-six albums and more than one hundred singles. He had acted in a few dozen films and exhibited his paintings widely in museums and galleries. He cowrote a Broadway show and developed an internet platform for creative content called BowieNet. He invented the Verbasizer, a sentence randomizer app for writing lyrics. By any standard, Bowie was wildly successful, both artistically and commercially. As a cultural icon, he achieved more than mere fame.

His creative quest wasn't always met with critical acclaim or financial gain, but he accepted the occasional lack of acceptance as a necessary condition of how he had decided to live: "People have either really accepted what I do, or they absolutely push it away," Bowie told an interviewer. "I didn't strive for success. I tried to do something artistically important."

His singular life was studded with innovation, and he practically invented reinvention. Where someone else might have rested in the glam rock Ziggy Stardust glory days, Bowie zagged with *Diamond Dogs* and then *Young Americans*. After that foray into soul, he left for Europe and experimental electronic music. Friend and collaborator Brian Eno explained Bowie's fearless shape-shifting as a way to "duck the momentum of a successful career" and keep his work fresh and interesting, for himself as much as for his audience. No doubt that one crucial common denominator—creating for himself, an audience of one—is what kept him a vital, timely, authentic artist right up until his death.

If you're in pursuit of pleasing others instead, it's easy to forget exactly why you initially started working on a creative endeavor. Bowie did not forget, saying:

> Never play to the gallery. Never work for other people in what you do. Always remember that the reason you initially started working was there was something inside yourself that, if you could manifest it, you felt you would understand more about yourself. I think it's terribly dangerous for an artist to fulfill other people's expectations.

Attempting to fulfill other people's expectations is a fool's errand when it comes to creative work.

It's inevitable that you will fail on some level, make compromises you regret, and end up with your worst work. You may or may not find acclaim but you'll be pretty miserable as a creative if you don't follow your heart. Bowie not only believed that, he embodied what it means to create for an audience of one.

**The ultimate paradox of creative work is that what you create for an audience of one is much more likely to reach an audience of millions.**

## CREATING FOR AN AUDIENCE OF ONE

Many creators dream of the day when millions of people will listen to their shows, read their books, buy their products, or watch them perform. But what will you bring to the table when you're performing only for an audience of one—yourself?

We tend to undervalue creating only for ourselves and overvalue creating for a huge audience. But your audience of one will be there every day when you wake up. If you think that you'll step it up only when the audience is larger, the audience paradoxically won't get any larger.

Most of what I create doesn't see the light of day. Over the course of a year I'll write close to 500,000 words. A minuscule fraction makes it into articles and books. By not sharing everything I make, I have freedom to play, to experiment, and to fail. I'm able to practice my art free of judgment, opinions of others, and expectations. I'm able to listen to myself and tap into an opportunity for full self-expression and self-exploration.

If you don't develop a regular practice of creating in private, the pressure to succeed becomes so great that you suffocate your creativity. In *Originals: How Non-Conformists Move the World*, Adam Grant found that people who had the most creative breakthroughs had a high volume of creative output. The cumulative output of any creative effort was more important to successful work than any individual piece of work. In private not only are we able to increase the volume of our creative output, but our creativity gets the space it needs to breathe, sing, and dance. It gets the space it needs to evolve from a mess into a masterpiece.

What you create in private often plants the seeds for your most resonant and impactful work, work that's ready for public consumption.

What we control in any creative endeavor is our effort, what we do each day to nurture our creativity, and our commitment to the process. Forget about the bestseller lists, the gallery openings, and the shining lights. The creation of fulfilling creative work is the result of losing yourself in the moment. When the work is done, your role comes to an end. The fate of a book, a film, a music album is ultimately out of your hands. You can't control how the world responds. But you can choose to appreciate and acknowledge your effort and simply start again. As author Ryan Holiday noted upon completion of one of his books:

> One of the hardest things to do is separate your work and the effort that you put in from the results. An actor doesn't control the movie around them. They don't control what the

other actors do. They don't control the marketing budget. They don't control the distribution. They could do the role of a lifetime, but the director or editor could mess it up in post-production. If your happiness with your job and your career is dependent on how the movie does at the box office, or how the critics respond to your role, you have placed your happiness with your own life in the hands of other people, and that's a recipe for profound disappointment.

While separating your work and effort from the results is one of the hardest things to do, it's also one of the most important. Otherwise, your sense of satisfaction, fulfillment, happiness, and overall well-being will fluctuate, depending on the "results." If the results are largely out of our control anyway, wouldn't we be better served by measuring our success by means that we have some control over? For example, are you proud of your work? Would you happily put your signature on it? Have you met or exceeded your own expectations or previous creation?

Our creativity speaks louder and more clearly when the work is separated from the results. Starting with the intention of fame and fortune drowns out the sound of our creativity and makes it more difficult for us to listen, resulting in a perpetual lack of fulfillment and an underappreciation of the joy we could experience through the process.

By reframing how we define "positive" outcomes, based on what we have control over, we increase the likelihood that our creative work will be rewarding.

## CREATIVE OUTCOMES

In the pursuit of success, the value of creativity for its own sake has diminished, if not disappeared entirely. While the internet and technology have made unparalleled amounts of creativity possible, they have ironically also inhibited the creative process. The predominant cultural narrative that drives so much creative work is "Why create if nobody will listen, pay, or pay attention? Why are we wasting our time?" We've placed celebrities on pedestals and turned their achievements and lifestyles into our new definition of success. The result is a profound sense of dissatisfaction with our creativity. Purity is lost in our work when everything we do is for some external outcome, when every creative pursuit unnecessarily turns professional.

But when you examine the most successful creators, almost none of them started out to gain fame, fortune, prestige, and accolades.

In the early 1990s a teen duo from France started making music from their bedrooms. Despite worldwide recognition of their music, you'd never recognize either member of Daft Punk if you saw them on the street. Rather than show their faces during their live performances, they wear robot masks. In a culture that puts "stars" on pedestals, celebrating fame and fortune, where people measure their self-worth in social media vanity metrics, it's unheard of that any artists would intentionally make themselves more anonymous as their popularity grows.

Grandiose fantasies often become the insidious motivator of so many aspiring creatives. But Daft Punk has an entirely different philosophy: "You don't need to be on the covers of magazines with your face to make good music."

Toward that end, when they were paid more than $300,000 for their performance at the Coachella music festival in 2006, nearly all of the money was put back into the performance, which raised the bar for what a live electronic music experience could be. It was a spectacle of light, sound, special effects, and music that eventually resulted in a YouTube video that went viral and got millions of views.

Despite having an audience of millions of adoring fans and opportunities with significant financial upsides, they've avoided the spotlight. For Daft Punk, it's always been about one thing: their love of making music. When we do anything for the love of the work itself, we are creating for an audience of one—or in Daft Punk's case, an audience of two.

Another creator, Maria Popova, founded *Brain Pickings*, a website that claims to be "an inventory of the meaningful life." It began as nothing more than a collection of links Popova emailed to seven friends. Today, it reaches millions of readers. Reflecting on its growth and success in her post about the lessons learned from ten years of running the site, Popova said:

> Those extrinsic motivators are fine and can feel life-affirming in the moment, but they ultimately don't make it thrilling to

get up in the morning and gratifying to go to sleep at night—and, in fact, they can often distract and detract from the things that do offer those deeper rewards.

To evaluate our efforts based solely on the extrinsic is the very opposite of what it means to listen to your deepest self. When we insist on the extrinsic, our work actually suffers. It's bled of its authenticity and its potential for an unmistakable signature, which ironically makes the possibility of external success less likely.

But these desires are natural. After all, we are living in an age of information overload that is defined by the ability to see everybody else's life and their creativity on perpetual display. Sharing creates the possibility of validation in the form of likes, comments, or whatever vanity metric your platform of choice is driven by. Not only is this validation fleeting, it's also toxic to creativity. We de-emphasize the joy of the process, compare ourselves to others, and become overly attached to outcomes. It's quite easy to get into the business of what *Life After Tampons* blog creator Jennifer Boykin describes as "comparing your insides to other people's outsides."

When we are envious, we give our energy and attention to what someone else has that we lack, thereby reinforcing a scarcity mind-set and cutting off the flow of creativity. Stop trying to become the next Beyoncé, Kanye, or Stephen King. The flaw in this desire is that you won't ever become—cannot become—the next version of that person. As a creator, your job is to commit to becoming the best version of you. If you're a better version of yourself today than you were yesterday, that's progress. Comparison and envy stand in the way of progress in any creative endeavor—or in any life, for that matter.

As Julia Cameron wisely points out in her iconic 1992 book *The Artist's Way*:

> Focused on the process, our creative life retains a sense of adventure. Focused on the product, the same creative life can feel foolish or barren.

""The Artist's Way' in an Age of Self-Promotion" is a 2016 *New Yorker* article by Carrie Battan, who writes:

> If I could, I would request an edition of "The Artist's Way" that speaks to twentysomethings, who've grown up online and then entered the so-called freelance economy, wherein workers are more likely to cobble together a piecemeal career of diverse gigs than secure nine-to-five jobs with benefits and opportunities for growth. In this economy, we're encouraged to think of units of time in dollar amounts, and to come up with inventive—creative, even—ways to monetize every last fledgling skill we possess.
>
> This life chafes against the lessons of "The Artist's Way," rendering them almost impossible to follow. Hobbies are now necessarily productive. If you're learning piano, you must try to record the jingle for that commercial your friend directed. If

you develop a curiosity about a niche topic, you must start an online newsletter dedicated to it, work to build your audience, and then try to monetize the newsletter. If you have a nice speaking voice, you must start a podcast. We're encouraged to be "goal-oriented" and rewarded with outsize praise for everything we've accomplished, and so we feel that we need to turn every creative pursuit into a professional one. This makes some of Cameron's lessons more urgent than ever. But, unlike earlier generations of readers, we don't need Cameron to protect us from the voices telling us to doubt ourselves. What we need, instead, are new voices granting us permission to try new things in private—and then leave them be.

This book is not about the value of creativity, but rather about the creative process itself. How can we find the joy of creating for creativity's sake again in a world that pushes us to focus on the external goals we can't control? Even if you do create to support yourself and your family, the process can still be fulfilling and joyous. My goal is to equip you with the habits, routines, rituals, and systems I've applied so you, too, can live a vibrant creative life unhindered by the modern pressure to monetize your art.

## MY PATH TO AN AUDIENCE OF ONE

As I became a creative full time, I dealt with the common struggles of being a creative in the twenty-first century. I craved fame, fortune, and external validation. I constantly compared myself to my peers. In many cases I didn't even see them as peers, but as people who were ahead of me because they had sold more books, had more fans, and reached a larger audience. But I eventually realized that my creativity combined with an obsession over outcomes created only madness, not meaning, as I found out when I first turned to writing as an adult. As I said before, the process was the point, not the potential external rewards.

My path to this revelation was long, as I didn't grow up immersed in creative habits. I often say, "I think God made a sorting error by giving me to my family." Other than my physical appearance and a few personality quirks, I don't feel like I have much in common with them, especially in terms of interests. On the surface, I don't come from what you might call a "creative" family.

- My father is a college professor in the agriculture department at UC Riverside.

- My sister is an anesthesiologist at the Veterans Affairs hospital in Santa Monica.

- My mother is a health worker for Riverside County.

But looking back, they were always taking photos, making home movies, mixing flavors and spices in the kitchen. No digital footprint. No recipes that can be replicated . . . just a collection of moments and memories that we will have to keep in our hearts and minds.

Despite my parents' creative outlets, we didn't engage in creative activities in my childhood. Our art projects and report cards were never put on the fridge. Math and science were always prioritized over other subjects in school. Turning to creativity solely for the sake of it took hold only much later in my life, a few weeks after college graduation. I wrote a sixty-three-page single-spaced autobiography in eight days to find meaning in an experience that had failed to live up to my expectations.

In writing my story, I hoped that perhaps I'd uncover elements of college that had been worthwhile and heal some of the wounds. Back then there were no blogs, and no way to share other than to email my posts to a few friends. But I found the process incredibly fulfilling. As Haruki Murakami said of his first writing efforts, "I was more interested in finishing it than whether or not it would ever see the light of day."

I continued to write to get through difficult periods in my life, eventually sharing my writing when blogs and social media became more common.

Early on, when I initially started to write, I felt compelled to share my ideas with the public because I wanted external validation, whether that was in the form of website traffic, a book deal, or words of affirmation. But as my creative life progressed over the years, I began to realize that true satisfaction came from the process, not the product.

## ABOUT THE BOOK

From the time I was seven years old I've had a special relationship with listening. It began with a Sony Walkman, a pair of Japanese silk pajamas, and an obsession with the music of Michael Jackson. The silk pajamas were about as close as I was getting to Michael Jackson's signature red leather jacket.

I listened endlessly to *Thriller* until the tape was so worn out that it no longer worked. In the sound of Michael's voice there was another world, one in which the impossible became possible, and a sense of magical realism, where imagination, curiosity, and the naive optimism that defines childhood intersected.

Several decades later, as a podcast host and interviewer, listening is my primary creative activity. The human voice has changed my life, and shaped and molded my own creative expression.

So as I was starting to think about this book, I had an epiphany that listening is the key to my creative process, and organizing content by what we listen to seemed inevitable and logical.

The creative process parallels listening—in fact, it is a form of listening: listening to ourselves and finding a desire to create without external pressure. It requires us to pay attention, to be alert to our environment, ourselves, other people, to stay open, engaged, and curious. To be alert to catch an expected—or unexpected—sound.

I've divided the book into four sections: how to listen to creativity, how to listen to yourself, how to listen to your environment, and how to listen to others constructively.

### Listening to Creativity

This section delves deeper into why creativity for creativity's sake—in lieu of creativity as a way to become rich, famous, praised, or successful—has a profound effect on who we are as people and how we live.

### Listening to Yourself

In order to reach a point where creation becomes its own reward, we have to shed our egos and detach from outcomes while remaining committed to the process. In a world where we're constantly inundated with a fire hose of input from a seemingly infinite array of sources, to foster our creativity we have to learn to listen to ourselves, to understand our own values, and have the courage to create what we want to exist, regardless of how the world responds.

### Listening to Your Environment

The environments that we inhabit affect us on a daily basis: everything from our physical space to the apps on our phone to the sounds we hear. By listening to our environments, we can deliberately design them to cultivate and maximize our creativity, making the experience pleasurable even if the actual act feels difficult at that moment.

## Listening to Others

In listening to others we prime our creative pump. In every creator's work, you'll find the echoes of those who have gone before them, the people they have been influenced and inspired by, and those whose work they've consumed. In addition to serving as sources of inspiration, others serve as support systems and creative collaborators.

Every creator's work is a mixture of the people they've spoken to, the books they've read, the art they've consumed, and the company they keep. However, it's extremely important to focus on the *right* kinds of influence, especially considering the way others can steer us to focus on the outcomes of creativity. What we put into that creative stew is entirely up to us. This section will arm you with tools to create an effective creative stew.

Within each of the four parts, you'll hear from three distinct sources:

○ My creative experience and process.

○ The guests on my podcast, *Unmistakable Creative*, whom I've interviewed and read about. I call them "Unmistakable Creatives."

○ Social-, behavioral-, and neuroscientists on creative habits.

To help you listen to your own unmistakable creative, I've provided more than a dozen activities and exercises. I think you'll find them intriguing, fun, and inspiring. I did them all myself and share the results here with you as examples: If I can do it, so can you.

To sit down each day and work on bringing ideas into existence that might inspire someone (even if it's only yourself) and that require time, effort, energy, and engagement . . . this is at the heart of what it means to be creative. The work becomes our source of questions, answers, and meaning. It challenges us, causes us to grow, energizes, revitalizes, reveals, and heals. Creativity is our oxygen supply. We don't wait for inspiration to strike. We don't wait until we're in the mood. We are disciplined, focused, persistent, and courageous. And we trust that if we show up, our muse will, too. It's not one piece of work, one moment in time, one burst of inspiration, but a daily practice and process that we are committed to for a lifetime.

Hollywood might tempt us to believe that a creative life is made of chaos-fueled occasional bursts of inspiration or what the writer Anne Lamott refers to as the "fantasies of the uninitiated." But the reality of a creative life is that it requires focus. Creativity is about showing up to make your "art," whatever it might be, a habit. It's an ongoing commitment to the process. It might be easy to forget this when we're bombarded with other voices telling us to think about rewards. As you read this book, I hope you'll hear the sound of someone whom you've long forgotten, your creative voice, just itching to shout out loud—and create the unmistakable.

## PART ONE

# LISTENING TO CREATIVITY

Writer Karan Bajaj's mother was a schoolteacher and his father was an engineer. As is common in Indian culture, he was supposed to become either a doctor or an engineer. He said, "For the first twenty-two years of my life I didn't think at all, I had no independent thought at all of who I wanted to be. I was just following the path that was laid out in front of me, which was get into engineering college, then business school, and become an engineer." But he started writing ten years ago at age twenty-eight, and published his first novel at twenty-nine.

In 2013, the film rights for his second novel were optioned and he signed a book contract for his third novel. Despite many people encouraging him to pursue his passion for writing in light of his success, he has kept his day job. He feels it is his dharma, or calling, to be in business. He told me in our conversation that not tying his passion to money was one of the best decisions he ever made. He said, "It's been very liberating for me to answer my deepest questions through my writing. I never write for my niche, my industry, my audience, my platform. In a sense I think that's been the reason for the success of my writing."

Bajaj's story is exemplary of the possibilities that open in our lives when we're willing to embrace creativity for its own sake rather than external recognition. The creative process—not the result—is the source of our happiness. We feel the joy of being so immersed and engaged in what we're doing that we lose track of time. We experience moments of creative daring, beautiful magic, and the unexpected surprises that show up along the way. Fortunately, our commitment to and belief in the process is entirely in our control. We can decide to show up, sit down, and create. If we listen to the process of creativity and stay attentive, it can be our gateway to meaning.

## THE DOWNSIDE OF REWARDS OVER PROCESS

Paradoxically, when we're excessively focused on potential rewards rather than the process, the product suffers.

○ If a podcaster is thinking about the potential downloads while conducting an interview, the quality of the interview declines. They're no longer present, conversations come across as canned, and they end up trying to sound impressive as opposed to inspiring or informative.

- If an author is thinking about reviews and bestseller lists while writing, the quality of their books declines. It places their focus on elements of creative work that are completely out of their control. What makes a great piece of writing great is an unwavering commitment to the craft, not the prize.

- If a musician is thinking about their potential Grammy Award while recording an album, the quality of the music suffers. They try to live up to other people's expectations and their work ends up feeling forced and inauthentic.

Somewhere in the middle of 2014, all of my work started to become about feeding my ego and getting external validation. I wanted the approval of my mentor, my audience, and the world at large. All I cared about was our bottom line. In that process the work I loved turned into the job I hated, and what had once been one of my greatest sources of joy was making me miserable.

We must learn to let go of our attachments and expectations if we're going to derive satisfaction from our work and create art that we're proud to put our signature on.

When we value product over process, we depart from what psychologist and author Carol Dweck calls a growth mind-set. With a growth mind-set, you believe that you can continue to grow and learn. With a fixed mind-set, any perceived flaws or strengths are seen as permanent. We believe our well-being is determined entirely by what's out of our control, and our motivation and effort all begin to dwindle.

Because of the rapid pace at which we can go from idea to execution in the digital world, this is an all too common occurrence for people who start creative projects on the internet. When an enthusiastic start doesn't translate into an overnight success, people give up on their creative work. They don't give their efforts enough time to experience any visible progress and inaccurately conclude that they lack the necessary creativity or talent. They overlook the fact that nearly every "overnight success" is usually years in the making.

When we focus on end results, we essentially defeat one of the main benefits of creative work: to derive joy from the work itself. Our well-being fluctuates based on the outcomes. If temporary setbacks appear permanent, any effort appears to be completely fruitless.

On the flip side, when we focus on the process, we see opportunities for improvement. Opportunities for improvement elicit action, effort, and enthusiasm. It's in "the thousands of days of trying, failing, sitting, thinking, resisting, dreaming, raveling, unraveling, that we are at our most engaged, alert, and alive," says Dani Shapiro, memoirist and author of *Still Writing: The Perils and Pleasures of a Creative Life*.

By sticking with the process, we also increase the likelihood of a favorable outcome or product.

Here's an example: When our content strategist, Kingshuk

Mukherjee joined the Unmistakable Creative team, his first major assignment was launching an interactive online course. Everything from the final product to the marketing and sales was based on his recommendations, but he had little control over the outcome (revenue generated from the launch). Reflecting on the launch, he said:

> You're taking on a new project and your results will dictate how much you get paid. Now, the more time you put into it, the more you have to lose. A bad outcome means not only will you not get paid, but you'll lose all the time you invested. So there I was writing three to four versions of a landing page, a bit more than I've ever taken on before. If I thought about how bad I need to nail the final version, I'd choke—I wouldn't perform at all. So instead, I looked at "What do I have to accomplish RIGHT NOW to make this project a win?"

He focused on the process and ultimately ended up with a successful outcome (an increase in revenue).

The process is in our control. The process results in progress, which in turn increases our motivation. External outcomes, on the other hand, are not. And if the only measure we have for our success is the external outcome, and we don't see it materializing, we're likely to give up or just get bored with the work.

If you see your creative work as a chore, an obligation, or solely as an item to cross off your to-do list, the work will feel that way to you and anybody who interacts with it. On the other hand, if you see your work as a gift, a privilege, an opportunity to share the truth of what's in your heart with the world, that's the experience you'll have with it. Same work, different perspectives.

For example, in 2003, Frank Warren, who had started a small business called Instant Information Systems, was in Paris when he had a powerful lucid dream about three postcards he had bought that day. Purely as a creative experiment, he was led to print three thousand anonymous stamped and self-addressed postcards, blank on one side. On the other side he listed some simple instructions to "anonymously share an artful secret they've never shared before." He handed them out to people randomly on the streets of Washington, D.C., not knowing what to expect. The idea went viral, and Frank started receiving postcards from thousands of people from around the world. "In a weird way, the secrets give me strength," he said in an interview on Mediabistro .com. Today PostSecret.com is the most visited advertisement-free site in the world with more than 200 million visitors. In addition to having no ads, no products can be purchased on *PostSecret*. As the absentee owner of Instant Information Systems, Warren has no need to monetize his creative endeavor.

In fact, based on *PostSecret*'s success, Warren has been able to raise awareness and money for a nonprofit suicide prevention organization. Warren is a clear example of the power of creativity for its own sake as well as giving back to others. When our work feels like a gift to others instead of an obligation, it gives us something to look forward to every day. It inspires us as much as it does the audience we create it for.

If outcomes become the primary way of measuring our creative success, and those outcomes are not to our liking, our creativity goes from being something that adds energy, joy, and enthusiasm to our life to something that drains it. We simply go through the motions, eventually losing our motivation.

LISTEN TO: **MADELEINE L'ENGLE**

But unless we are creators we are not fully alive. What do I mean by creators? Not only artists, whose acts of creation are the obvious ones of working with paint or clay or words. Creativity is a way of living life, no matter our vocation or how we earn our living. Creativity is not limited to the arts, or having some kind of important career.

## THE MYTH OF "MAKING IT"

When my self-published book *The Art of Being Unmistakable* gained the attention of media pundit Glenn Beck, I was suddenly in the spotlight like I'd never been before. My book was selling thousands of copies, I was receiving checks from Amazon far larger than anything I'd ever imagined, and it felt like I could do no wrong. But a few months later, everything was back to normal. I was confronted with the next challenge: letting go of my ego-driven desire for external validation and getting back to work like none of this had ever happened.

The myth of "making it" causes many aspiring creatives to believe that there will be a day when they no longer have to do the work that has gotten them to where they are. Those who buy into this myth and rest on their laurels become victims of their own success. They don't stand the test of time.

For instance, author and journalist Jonah Lehrer was on track to have a prolific career. He was a regular contributor at major media outlets like *Wired* magazine, had written multiple books, and was a frequent keynote speaker. However, it surfaced that he had put made-up Bob Dylan quotes in one of his books, and he was eventually outed as a "serial fabricator." Lehrer later described his career as a "mixture of insecurity and ambition" that led him to stop doing the original creative work that had gotten him to where he was in the first place. He became a victim of his own success.

As author Ryan Holiday said to me in an interview on *The Unmistakable Creative*, success gives you the conditional opportunity to try again. We have to begin every new creative endeavor with the same enthusiasm and commitment regardless of the results from our previous efforts.

The act of creation contains a sense of fulfillment that we'll never get from any fleeting external outcome. Consider: A book on the *New York Times* bestseller list this week may be forgotten by next week. The box office smash eventually becomes a footnote. Today's viral sensation has vanished by the time you wake up tomorrow.

When we are dependent on anything external to fuel our creativity, we're effectively handing over control of our lives and happiness to that external reward. When the reward vanishes, so, too, does our creativity.

Our creativity can provide us with something to look forward to every day and a lasting sense of fulfillment. Why is the creative process itself so fulfilling?

LISTEN TO: SARAH JOY SHOCKEY

**Anything you create that brings you joy or even frustration shapes you into someone with experience.**

## CREATIVITY MAKES US HAPPY

The idea that creativity increases happiness isn't just a theory or an artsy opinion: A number of research studies have proved a strong link between creativity and happiness.

In our formal education system, creativity is primarily seen as an extracurricular activity, yet students derive tremendous benefit from a curriculum that includes the arts.

In 2014, University of North Carolina at Greensboro professor of psychology Paul Silvia and his colleagues published a paper called "Everyday Creativity in Daily Life: An Experience-sampling Study of 'Little C' Creativity." Their thesis was that "everyday creativity—creative actions that are common among ordinary people in daily life, such as drawing, making recipes, writing, and any activity done with the purpose of being creative—both fosters and reflects psychological health."

Seventy-nine college students participated in the weeklong study, in which they were asked whether they were doing something creative and to describe their emotional state at the moment. When participants were being creative, they reported feeling significantly happier and more active. Everyday creativity "allows people to explore their identities, form new relationships, cultivate competence, and reflect critically on the world. In turn, the new knowledge, self-insight, and relationships serve as sources of strength and resilience."

LISTEN TO: **DAVID BOWIE**

**I've become more and more selfish about what it is I want to do, what I find satisfying. Because if you make yourself happy, a little bit of that sunshine can spread onto others.**

You might assume that you have to be a capital-A artist, painter, or poet "creative genius" in order to benefit from the creativity-happiness connection. But as *Pacific Standard* staff writer Tom Jacobs noted in his analysis of the Greensboro study, "you don't have to be a master poet or painter to reap the emotional rewards."

Creativity, it turns out, doesn't just contribute to our happiness but also to our mental and physical health. Expressing ourselves creatively is a form of self-care in many ways. It gives us the opportunity for self-reflection. And as we build our creative skills, we build confidence. Many therapists even prescribe creative expression to their patients for healing purposes.

For instance, in a study called "How Art Changes Your Brain," twenty-eight people between the ages of sixty-two and seventy were "encouraged to produce visual art and find their own forms of personal expression." During the ten-week study, an art educator introduced drawing and painting methods and materials, which allowed the participants to experiment however they wished.

Such visual art interventions, which were designed to test how art could affect aging, resulted in:

- Reduced distress

- Increased self-reflection

- Normalized heart rate, blood pressure, and cortisol levels

A study of Mindfulness Based Art Therapy (MBAT), a method that integrates mindfulness meditation skills and aspects of art therapy into an eight-week program for women with cancer, produced similar results. Participants in the study experienced significant decreases in symptoms of distress (anxiety, depression, hostility, and obsessive-compulsive tendencies) and significant improvements in key aspects of health-related quality of life (physical functioning, bodily pain, and mental health).

The incremental creative steps we take each day keep us

moving forward on our unmistakable path. We discover and reinforce the link between our happiness and our creativity. For instance, my father is a prolific photographer with no presence on Instagram and a Facebook page on which he hardly ever shares his photos. When I asked him about his love for photography, my dad simply said, "I always was just interested in photography. In high school I joined a photography club. I wanted a hobby and I realized this was a great hobby." But I think it was more than just a hobby. Photography gave him a way to preserve some of his most cherished memories, like the countries he visited and the children he watched grow up.

LISTEN TO: **DAVID BOWIE**

**If you feel safe in the area you're working in, you're not working in the right area. Always go a little further into the water than you feel you're capable of being in.**

My mother is an incredibly gifted cook with no desire to start a food blog, food truck, or restaurant and seems content with serving our family. My mother's love for cooking stemmed from a similar motivation as my father's photography: "Even though I never cooked growing up," she said, "I wanted to preserve generations of recipes. Your dad loved good food and cooking for our family has always given me a great deal of happiness."

Creativity can even help people heal from traumatic events.

A study conducted by University of Texas psychologist James Pennebaker revealed that writing about traumatic experiences can have a healing effect. Participants in the study were asked to write about their deepest thoughts and most traumatic experiences for three to five consecutive days for fifteen to thirty minutes at a time.

The participants in Pennebaker's study experienced:

- Long-term improvements in mood and indicators of well-being compared to participants writing about control topics

- Beneficial influences on immune function, including t-helper cell growth, antibody response to Epstein-Barr virus, and antibody response to hepatitis B vaccinations

- Improvements in grades

- Finding new jobs more quickly after layoffs and writing about the experience

The science clearly indicates that creativity can serve as a powerful cure for trauma and an aid to our happiness and overall well-being. Whether it's recovering from the loss of a loved one or the end of a romantic relationship, or just searching for clarity on the next chapter of our lives, creativity can help us become happier and more resilient.

# CREATIVITY CAN INCREASE PRODUCTIVITY

The link between creativity and happiness is a bit like the chicken and the egg: Creativity makes us happier and our happiness increases our creativity.

Teresa Amabile, Harvard professor and author of *The Progress Principle,* teaches a course on managing for creative professionals in the business world. Over ten years, she and her colleagues looked at what makes people happy, motivated, productive, and creative at work. They asked dozens of creative professionals to submit a daily electronic diary about whatever creative project they were working on. Participants answered questions about their emotions and the events of the day, what Amabile and her colleagues refer to as "inner work life."

Their first discovery was that "when people are feeling most deeply and happily engaged in their work, they're more likely to be creatively productive." The second discovery, known as "the progress principle," revealed that "the #1 driver of positive inner work life was making progress in meaningful work, even if that progress was a small win." Every day we make progress in really small ways, but we have a tendency to overlook minor accomplishments because we're so obsessed with major ones. This skews our perception of our progress. But if we get in the habit of tracking small wins, we can change that perception, build up our momentum, and make progress on our most meaningful work.

A small win could be hitting your daily word count as a writer or receiving an appreciative comment on your art. It could be fixing a line of code in software that you're writing. All of our small wins eventually add up, resulting in creative momentum.

An ongoing commitment to our creativity, a daily practice, regardless of what form it takes, enables us to experience progress. When we experience progress, we gain creative momentum and productivity. As a result, we can reach a state called "flow" or "deep work" more readily, which increases our happiness. Our brains are wired to crave this state of flow. It's when there's no place you'd rather be and nothing else you'd rather be doing. It's the feeling I get when I catch a perfect wave and the world around me disappears. Flow is a state in which we are singularly focused on the task at hand, our senses heighten, and we lose track of time. The activity itself becomes the reward.

LISTEN TO: **BRENÉ BROWN**

**We are born makers, and creativity is the ultimate act of integration—it is how we fold our experiences into our being.**

Flow puts us into a state of almost unparalleled joy. The process becomes so intrinsically rewarding that we're able to easily detach from the outcome. Flow not only makes time fly by, but leads to disproportionate increases in creative output. What usually might take two hours takes thirty minutes when we are in flow. I've seen this pattern over and over in my life as a writer.

This kind of deep immersion creates a rhythm and momentum that feels so good that the creative process becomes addictive.

If you do happen to succeed by external standards, remember that creative success is an infinite game, one that we "play to play instead of play to win," according to Seth Godin. If you maintain a consistent creative practice, there may come a point where you're making your art for more than just an audience of one. It's inevitable that when your work reaches a wider audience, you'll face criticism and even envy from others. In these moments, it's important that you don't let external success become the source of your joy and fulfillment. Otherwise your happiness is in the hands of something over which you have no control.

Financial or critical success allows you to keep playing that creative game, but it doesn't make you any happier than the game itself. The greatest reward you'll derive from external success is the opportunity to keep doing your work, and that is the ultimate gift of creativity.

LISTEN TO: LADY GAGA

When you make music or write or create, it's really your job to have mind-blowing, irresponsible, condomless sex with whatever idea it is you're writing about at the time.

# PART TWO

# LISTENING
# TO
# YOURSELF

When your art is not your way of earning a living, you have a sense of freedom to create whatever you're proud to put your signature on, even if it doesn't have the potential to pay the bills. The downsides to your creative risks are minimal because you can create whatever you want.

This is the artistic equivalent of childhood: the opportunity to experience creative effort as play rather than work. In this beautiful and special time, you're liberated from the expectations of others and have an uninhibited freedom of expression. When there's no audience, you can truly dance like nobody's watching and sing like nobody's listening.

But when we seek approval from others and let them set a standard we feel compelled to meet, we stop listening to ourselves. We understand that people have opinions of us, so we dedicate our efforts to making those opinions favorable. The quirks that make us fascinating get buried under a validation-inspired facade. We tell ourselves that what we've created is a compromise, but sadly what we've compromised is our core values.

To learn to listen to ourselves, we need to restore our true creativity, not make it up from scratch.

Unmistakable Creative Sally Hogshead struggled with finding her creative voice. As the baby of her family, she "tend[ed] to be creative and nontraditional" in a family where her two siblings cast a large shadow (an older brother graduated from Harvard and a sister won three Olympic gold medals in swimming). She wanted to figure out how she could stand out creatively. Her father said, "You don't have to *change* who you are. You have to become *more* of who you are." But many of us seem to turn into *less* of who we are as we navigate the "real" world. Ultimately we have to learn to listen to our own instincts, intuition, and creative impulses.

Learning to listen to yourself begins with questioning what you're told. For so many of us, we simply accept what we're being told about ourselves and our work. If we're told we're not creative, we might assume it's true. If we're told that our work is no good, we might get discouraged and give up. When we make such assumptions, we see both our reality and creative capacity as fixed. However, when we start to question what people have told us, our creativity becomes much more fluid.

The courage to ask daring questions and challenge superficial answers, and the willingness to accept resonant answers, allows us to discover what we're being called to create. Your creativity starts to sound louder and louder and the song it sings is more truly your own. But what questions will unearth your true self? What do you need to do? Trust yourself, listen to your values, learn to be present, and cultivate solitude.

## TRUST YOURSELF

I've looked back at creative projects that didn't live up to my expectations or even failed, and realized it was all due to not having the courage to trust myself. I kept looking to everyone around me for answers and allowed them to guide every decision I made.

This is what we do when we place other people on a pedestal and overvalue their opinions about us and our work. It's only when you return to trusting yourself and your own instincts, that you regain creative momentum.

As Steven Pressfield wrote in his book *Turning Pro,* "When we project a quality or virtue onto another human being, we ourselves almost always already possess that quality, but we're afraid to embrace (and to live) that truth." Discovering our own truth and embracing it begins with evaluating our values.

## LISTEN TO YOUR VALUES

There's no shortage of advice in the modern world. Podcasts, blogs, self-help books, and more have infiltrated our consciousness. This barrage of advice makes us constantly trade one definition of success for another. One day it's writing a bestseller. The next it's aspiring to be in the history books among the elite in our field. Yet we still find ourselves dissatisfied because we haven't lived up to what we delude ourselves into thinking is *our* new definition of success.

We've bought into the notion that if you do exactly what somebody in a position of authority tells you, you will get the promised result, despite plenty of evidence to the contrary. This is the great fallacy of authority and influence. When we do anything that's out of alignment with our values, even if we succeed, it will feel like a failure because it wasn't true to our hearts. The easiest thing to forget is that the people who influenced our values won't be the ones to live with the consequences of whatever choices we make.

**In the simplest of terms, our values are determined by whatever it is that we choose to make the highest priority in our lives and why we choose to do something.** Money, fame, time, freedom, and opportunity for self-expression are all examples of values.

For example, in choosing guests for *The Unmistakable Creative* podcast, I always value how interesting a person's story is over how famous or successful they are. Years ago when I interviewed author Simon Sinek about discovering my purpose for what I did, he said, "You're obsessed with people who are good at unusual things." The people I interview are the clearest expression of that purpose.

Writer AJ Leon valued his opportunity for self-expression above money and fame. When he didn't like the direction his publisher was forcing him to go with his book, he returned his advance and published *The Life and Times of a Remarkable Misfit* as a free digital collection of essays. After it was downloaded more than 100,000 times, he launched a Kickstarter campaign for a physical version of the book that was fully funded within four hours.

Unmistakable Creative guest Nisha Moodley, who works with women in finding internal and emotional freedom in their lives through coaching and retreats, values "how [she wants] people to feel when they come into [her] world" to describe the design of her website. She's a stickler for typos, doesn't want the website experience to feel clunky, and wants all of the details of working with her to feel seamless. The details are all about making her customers and clients feel a certain way.

But to me her statement applies to more than the design of a website. It's a deliberate decision to ensure that her work is an unmistakable expression of her values.

Listening to your values can not only amplify the impact of your work, but can also help you to find greater levels of joy and fulfillment in the process. From 2009 to 2013 the podcast that our listeners know today as *The Unmistakable Creative* was called *BlogcastFM*. At the end of 2013, we decided to change the name and massively overhaul the brand. Our biggest fans thought we were completely out of our minds. They thought it made no sense to change what they deemed such a "good name."

But I wanted it to be more creative, visually appealing, and provocative with a purpose. When people came into our world or landed on our website for the first time, I wanted it to be loud and clear that this was a place unlike any other on the internet: unmistakable. *The Unmistakable Creative* was born, and today we have a fan base of both listeners and guests who love our brand far more than they ever did when it was called *BlogcastFM*. Listening to ourselves while having the courage and conviction to create what we wanted to see exist in the world has led to a much more resonant and impactful body of work.

LISTEN TO: **MAYA ANGELOU**

**We write for the same reason that we walk, talk, climb mountains or swim the oceans—because we can. We have some impulse within us that makes us want to explain ourselves to other human beings. That's why we paint, that's why we dare to love someone—because we have the impulse to explain who we are.**

Listening to our values also makes the work more personal and, ultimately, more rewarding. If the work you do doesn't excite you, if it doesn't make you feel something, then it's a tall order to expect that it will do the same for someone else.

Take über–Unmistakable Creative Oprah. Shortly after her popularity started to surge, the competition began to pay attention. Sensationalist talk show hosts like Jerry Springer and Geraldo Rivera started doing whatever they could to raise their ratings. Oprah listened to herself, deliberately ignoring her competitors, and created a show she was proud to put her name on.

Her show "elevated itself out of the heap of trash TV to a show that intentionally embraced spirituality and positivity." Oprah's work made the lives of millions of women around the world better because she didn't compromise her values.

## UNCOVER YOUR VALUES

To listen to yourself means to do creative work that's in alignment with your own values. Decide who you want to be and what you want to create. Answer the following questions to explore your own values. I've put in my answers as examples:

**How do you want people to feel when they come into your world?**

*When people listen to* The Unmistakable Creative, *I want them to feel that they've landed somewhere unlike anywhere else on the internet, a place that gets their creative juices flowing.*

**What makes you angry?**

*Nothing makes me angrier than people who bury their own creativity by simply imitating other people's creations. This is the central ethos of our Unmistakable Creative brand.*

**What lights you up?**

*People who have found unusual and interesting ways to express their creativity light me up.*

If you take time to reflect on these questions, despite their simplicity, you'll find your answers to be quite revealing.

Another way to discover your values is to write a personal manifesto. In his book *Louder Than Words*, Todd Henry encourages readers to consider the following questions:

**What change do you want to see in the world through your work?**

*The change I hope to see in the world through my work at Unmistakable Creative is a radical transformation of education. I would like to see an education system that isn't driven simply by grades and test scores, but instead takes into account multiple forms of intelligence and places a higher value on creativity. I'd like to see more and more people able to earn their living from doing work that they love.*

**What is the message that's burning so intensely that you corner others and force them to listen to you ramble on about it at a dinner party?**

*I want my work to give people the tools necessary to achieve personal excellence in every area of their lives, from their work to their relationships to their health.*

Use these questions as a compass, but draw your own map.

# LEARN TO BE PRESENT

Sometimes signs from the universe can revolutionize our creativity. But unless we're fully present, we can easily overlook these signs and miss out on amazing opportunities.

For example, poet Molly Peacock saw an exhibit of paper flower collages in New York when she was in her thirties. Though struck by their beauty, she forgot about them soon after. Twenty years later, she chanced upon an image of a similar exhibit in London. By then she knew she had to learn more about the artist and embarked on a combination biography and memoir called *The Paper Garden: An Artist Begins Her Life's Work at 72*. Peacock's subject, Mary Delany, noticed a falling geranium petal in 1772. In a flash of presence and inspiration, she cut out a tissue paper replica of the petal . . . and then the whole flower. In the remaining sixteen years of her life, she created more than a thousand paper "mosaics." All of this came about because both women were present enough to notice the beauty around them.

A lack of presence can be counterproductive to whatever it is we want to achieve in the future. I was an intern at Intuit's TurboTax group the summer between my first and second year of business school, and I was obsessed with ensuring that my internship led to a job offer. When I asked one of the senior executives at a "lunch and learn" what it took to rise quickly, she said being present in the moment was key. Despite her advice, I remained preoccupied with getting an offer at the end of the summer, which resulted in the internship's ending without the offer I wanted. Since then, the idea of presence has echoed in my ears.

"Presence" as a way of getting ahead in your career flies in the face of the linear achievement-oriented approach to life that we are conditioned into adopting. Our eyes are perpetually on the proverbial prize of the promotion, the higher paycheck, the next accolade, or the next achievement rather than the moment right in front of us.

When we are not present in the moment, our performance declines. This sentiment was echoed by Michael Bloomberg in his autobiography *Bloomberg by Bloomberg*:

> Young people starting their careers today are too impa-tient for current compensation, at the expense of continuing their education and giving their jobs a chance. Get back to work. Forget the money today. There's plenty of time for that later.

The paths of people who have rewarding creative lives are al-most never linear, and those who are the most present appear to have the most prolific pasts and abundant futures.

Dwelling on the past and worrying about the future pro-duces false narratives that drown out the sound of our most authentic voice. When we're present, we're fully engaged in whatever we're doing. When we're not present, we either do not create or what we do create feels safe, manufactured, and inauthentic.

## LET GO OF JUDGMENT

There's a natural tendency to judge our early artistic efforts, which Julia Cameron describes as "artistic abuse." When we judge our work while we're creating it, we're no longer present by definition. The creative mind cannot be the critical mind simultaneously. Thomas Sterner, author of *The Practicing Mind,* made a subtle but powerful distinction in an interview on *The Unmistakable Creative.* Whatever our creative habit is, we can decide whether it's a day of learning or a day of performance. During the process of learning we'll struggle and make mistakes. And during performance, we play or create at the top of our game. By letting go of our judgment and not performing every single day, we're able to focus on the here and now.

- We're not thinking about the next chapter of the book, but the sentence we're currently writing.

- We're not thinking about the standing ovation at the end of a performance, but the measure or scales we're currently playing.

Most of our judgments about our work tend to involve the past or the future. We dwell on how our work might have been criticized in the past, or worry about how people might react to it in the future. They're largely driven by external influences. Staying fully in the present allows us to reduce the judgment we bring to our work. One of the easiest mind-set shifts that allows us to become present is the core thesis of this book: Work for an audience of one, yourself. When the only person you're trying to please is yourself, judgments vanish, and in that process we become more present. With presence we achieve flow, reinforcing the cycle of pleasure we derive from our creativity.

With our judgments silenced, we're able to hear the sound of our own creative voices more clearly—and in the present.

## CULTIVATE SOLITUDE

We rarely leave our homes without our phones in hand. We get in our cars and immediately call someone or turn on music to fill the silence. In that process, the sound of our own creative voice competes with everything else for our attention.

By cultivating solitude, we're able to turn down the volume on everything else in our lives and find enough silence for the sound of our creative voice. Entrepreneur Brian Scudamore wrote a piece on *Medium* titled "Why Successful People Spend 10 Hours a Week Just Thinking." Often "thinking," or what I call solitude, can feel unproductive. Many people struggle with solitude because it can make us feel bored, lonely, and as though we're doing nothing.

LISTEN TO: **HILARY MANTEL**

If you get stuck, get away from your desk. Take a walk, take a bath, go to sleep, make a pie, draw, listen to music, meditate, exercise; whatever you do, don't just stick there scowling at the problem. But don't make telephone calls or go to a party; if you do, other people's words will pour in where your lost words should be. Open a gap for them, create a space. Be patient.

When we are sitting in solitude, the silence can be ironically deafening. We think to ourselves, "One harmless peek online won't kill me." We go through our cycle of checking email, Facebook, and Twitter. Wash, rinse, repeat. Over a long enough time line, harmless check-ins flush creative careers down the toilet. Author Steven Pressfield calls such self-sabotage "resistance."

While writing this book, I struggled with carving out solitude and encountered resistance. I procrastinated by chatting with friends online, and in some cases I even skipped entire writing days. Despite having finished a previous manuscript in six months, I worried that for the first time I might actually miss a deadline. The myth of resistance is that the artists and creators who have conquered it have permanently defeated it. But resistance is drawn to significant creative endeavors like a moth to a flame. It comes back with a vengeance.

The search for the silver bullet that allows us to defeat resistance is a fool's errand. There's no silver bullet. The work itself defeats resistance. It was sitting in a coffee shop unplugged from the rest of the world that enabled me to overcome resistance and embrace the solitude.

If we're willing to sit quietly, slow down, and reflect, solitude can serve as a pathway to creative insight.

There are a number of simple ways that we can cultivate more solitude in our lives.

## MEDITATE

You don't have to join a monastery or become a Buddhist to build a meditation practice. You don't have to purchase crystals or candles or blow a whole paycheck at a new age gift shop. You don't have to even sit in a room for thirty minutes each day with your eyes closed. All you have to do is spend two or three minutes to reap the benefits. It's not the length of your meditation practice but the frequency that is beneficial. With an ongoing meditation practice, the incessant chatter of your mind starts to become quieter and the sound of your authentic voice becomes clearer.

## READ A PHYSICAL BOOK

Reading is a solitary pursuit, and as an added bonus, it's a period of solitude in which you learn something. Pick up any book off your shelf and read twenty pages or so for twenty minutes. By reading a book, you plant creative seeds that will serve as inspiration throughout the rest of your day. "Fill your ears with the music of good sentences, and when you finally approach the page yourself, the music will carry you," says author Dani Shapiro. This is why it's incredibly useful to read before you write.

## WRITE IN A JOURNAL

Journals and sketchbooks are essential tools for creating in private. The daily act of writing three pages longhand was popularized by Julia Cameron in her book *The Artist's Way*. The goal is not to sound smart or clever, but to clear and quiet the mind. Sarah Peck, swimmer, designer, and writer, described this process as follows:

> In my own life, I spend a lot of time writing. I try to write every single day. I get up in the morning, and I write a couple of pages. It's just chicken scratch. Some mornings, I'm writing an ode to how much I want my coffee. It's so bad. I'm writing, "Coffee, coffee, coffee, coffee, coffee. Am I done yet? Did I get there?" I'm just whining on the page. And other mornings, it's to-do lists because I wake up in such an urgency and adrenaline-fueled state. "Oh, my God. I have so much to do. I'm not gonna be able to do it." I'm really panicked. I just literally write a to-do list. And it cleanses your brain. It's like just

a little wash. It gets some of that junk and that garbage off. And then I get to think a little clearer through the day.

I start every morning by writing anywhere between three and four pages in a Moleskine notebook. By writing in a physical notebook, I'm able to set aside time for self-reflection, free from the perpetual buzz of being connected. Writing by hand forces me to slow down, causing me to become more attentive and mindful of my inner voice. And it results in a singular focus, which is a critical ingredient and precursor to achieving flow.

Physical notebooks also provide us with something that no app or digital tool can. Former Moleskine PR director Erik Fabian said they give us "a platform for the imagination." The beauty of a physical notebook is that its constraints breed creativity. When we're using nothing but pen and paper, we're able to imagine things far beyond the limitations of what's possible within our digital tools.

In his book *Presentation Zen*, Garr Reynolds tells the following story about a senior designer at Apple:

Most designers who've grown up on computers usually do much of their planning and brainstorming on pen and paper. This became very clear to me one day at Apple when I visited a senior director for one of the creative teams on the other side of the Apple campus to get his input on the project we were working on. He said he had sketched out a lot of ideas that he wanted to show me. I assumed that he had prepared some slides or a movie or at least printed out some color images in Illustrator or Photoshop to show me. But when I arrived at his office, I found that his beautiful Apple Cinema Display on his desk was off (I learned later that this talented creative director worked for days without ever turning on his Mac).

Nearly every prolific creator seems to share the habit of carrying a notebook.

Vincent van Gogh, Pablo Picasso, and Ernest Hemingway all used notebooks. Beethoven "saved everything in a series of notebooks" and "had notebooks for rough ideas, notebooks for improvements on those ideas and notebooks for finished ideas," says Twyla Tharp.

We usually don't have a shortage of ideas, but instead we lack the discipline to capture those ideas. A notebook helps us to develop that discipline. Jotting down ideas in notebooks is a bit like putting messages in bottles or planting seeds. We don't know when our messages will reach the person they're intended to reach or when they'll bear fruit. Regardless of your art form, a notebook can benefit your creative practice tremendously.

Our journals and sketchbooks give us an opportunity to ask *ourselves* questions and explore the answers. Our curiosity can also extend beyond the pages of journals and notebooks.

## CURIOSITY AND QUESTIONS

Curiosity is one of the most important traits you can cultivate to learn to listen to yourself and fuel your creativity. "Discovery is predicated on curiosity. The more curious you are, the more willing you will be to engage in each new experience. The easiest way to tap into your natural curiosity is by asking questions," says Tina Seelig in her book *Insight Out*.

If you have children, you may have noticed that they seem to be in a perpetual state of curiosity. They ask "why" about a hundred times a day, often to the point of driving you crazy. You might even remember your parents getting so fed up with the question that the answer to everything was "because" followed by no actual explanation.

There's a tremendous power in asking questions. Questions don't just give us answers, they also force us to examine what we're hearing for meaning, purpose, and significance. Questions are our pathway to innovation, creativity, and insight. They enable us to listen to and learn about ourselves and engage in a deep exploration of our values. They reignite our childlike curiosity.

In his TED talk, former Google software engineer Matt Cutts advocates a simple approach to cultivating curiosity: Try something new for thirty days. We all have a list of things that we've always wanted to try but haven't gotten around to:

- Sign up for a circus arts class.

- Build something with your hands (i.e., a new piece of furniture or clothing).

- Try an action adventure sport like rock climbing or kite surfing.

○ Start a public works art project like Candy Chang's *Before I Die* walls, where people write what they want to do before they die on one of two thousand walls around the world.

○ Work on a DIY project like making a drone. On the website DIYdrones.com, you can make a military-strength drone for 1 percent of the cost of buying one yourself.

For Cutts, his thirty-day challenges—which included taking a picture every day, writing a novel, and giving up sugar—caused his confidence to grow and made him go "from desk-dwelling computer nerd to the kind of guy who bikes to work for fun."

Your approach to developing your curiosity doesn't need to be as audacious or ambitious as Cutts's. It could be as simple as taking a different route home from work or shopping at a different grocery store than usual. Make a list of all the places in your hometown that you've always wondered about but have never been to. Visit one each week. Document the experience by making some art about it. Be curious about yourself and your reaction to your new adventures.

## WHAT DO YOU NEED TO CREATE? LISTENING TO YOUR BODY

Part of listening to yourself means listening to your body. It's hard to be at your best creatively when you're not at your best physically. Creative habits require energy. Energy comes from proper self-care in the form of sleep, nutrition, and exercise. Without adequate amounts of all three, you are at a self-imposed handicap and you can't sustain peak creativity.

## SLEEP

One of our unhealthy cultural narratives is the bragging rights that come with how many hours we've worked. It's not uncommon for start-up founders and employees to work eighty to one hundred hours a week. But the decline in cognitive performance that occurs when we work these hours in lieu of sleep is well documented. "We sacrifice sleep in the name of productivity, but ironically, our loss of sleep, despite the extra hours we put in at work, adds up to more than eleven days of lost productivity," says the author of *The Sleep Revolution,* Arianna Huffington.

In addition to a decline in cognitive performance, sleep deprivation can lead to major mental health issues like anxiety and depression. My own battle with depression, which I described in my previous book, was caused largely by sleep deprivation. A lack of sleep is more toxic to our well-being than a lack of food or water. No one can be very creative when sleep-deprived.

So perhaps the most underrated creative hack is sleep. It has a profound impact and serves a number of functions that go beyond creativity.

"When we fall asleep, our bodies shift into maintenance mode and devote themselves to storing energy, fixing or replacing damaged cells, and growing, while our brains clean out toxins, process the day's experiences and sometimes work on problems that have been occupying our waking minds," says Alex Soojung-Kim Pang in his book *Rest: Why You Get More Done When You Work Less.*

LISTEN TO: **IRA GLASS**

**When you start in a new field, your work won't be as good as your taste. It will take years for your taste and the quality of your work to intersect. Failure is essential. There's no substitute for it. It's not just encouraged but required.**

Adequate sleep can lead to significant productivity gains and creative breakthroughs. In her book on sleep, Arianna Huffington cites a study that Cheri Mah from the Stanford Sleep Disorders Clinic conducted on the Stanford varsity men's basketball team, titled "The Effects of Sleep on Athletic Performance."

Mah recorded the team's normal sleep patterns—they averaged just more than six and a half hours each night—along with statistics on sprints, free throws, and three-point shots. Then, for five to seven weeks, she had them aim for a minimum of ten hours in bed each night, spending as much of the time as possible asleep. The players' sleep average went up to eight and a half hours, and the increases in performance were dramatic. Sprint times were 0.7 seconds faster, free-throw shooting went up by 9 percent, and three-point shooting increased by 9.2 percent.

The study makes clear that a good night's sleep can lead to a dramatic increase in peak performance. If elite athletes like members of the Stanford men's basketball team are tapping into its power, why don't we all take advantage of sleep? When your body is telling you it needs rest, listen to your body and give it what it's craving.

## SLEEPING LIKE A BABY

What if you want to sleep more but you're having trouble falling and staying asleep? Dozens of books have been devoted to this subject (see Resources for a few of the best), but I have developed a few tips that address our generation's plugged-in tendencies.

- If you're an iPhone user, use the night shift mode, and set your phone to automatically adjust its screen to a lower brightness level two or three hours before your bedtime.

- Try to avoid screens at least one hour before bed. Whatever productivity gains you think you're making by responding to one last email, you'll more than make up for by avoiding screens one hour before you go to sleep.

- Devices in the bedroom are double-edged swords because some people use their phones as alarm clocks. A potential work-around to this is to connect your phone to a Bluetooth speaker; you'll still hear the alarm go off, but you won't have to keep your device in the room.

- Consider using an essential oils diffuser. According to an article on Prevention.com, researchers monitored the sleep cycles of thirty-one men and women with brain scans, and "on the night they whiffed the lavender herb, subjects slept more soundly; they also felt more energetic the next morning." In my own experience, the scent of lavender tends to be incredibly soothing and leads to great sleep.

## SLEEP, DREAMS, AND THE SUBCONSCIOUS MIND

I think you should never go to bed at night without giving a request to your subconscious. You might not have noticed that the content of your dreams is often similar to whatever information you were exposed to prior to sleeping. (Hence the reason one of my mentors warned that right before bed wasn't a good time to watch Jack Bauer attempting to defuse a nuclear bomb.)

You may also have noticed that when you're stuck on a problem, you seem to have figured it out when you wake up in the morning. Fortunately, we can tap into this power as a method of creative problem solving. Prior to going to bed, make a request to your subconscious mind:

- If it's a stand-up routine you're struggling to finish, ask for ideas that will help you to complete it.

- If you're trying to come up with music lyrics, ask for a phrase that will help you write your songs.

- If you're a computer programmer stuck on a line of code, ask for a bug fix.

- If you're attempting to increase your business revenue, ask for a new product or service idea.

When you wake up in the morning, write whatever comes to mind in a notebook. Don't worry if it's not the exact answer to your question. I've found that once I actually start writing, the answers to my questions are somehow revealed.

Listening to your dreams can also be a direct catalyst for creative work. I know a poet who had such a vivid dream after her mother died that she "saw" it as a film. She dreamed of making a film of her dream for ten years. Eventually she took filmmaking courses at a local media center, found actors, and made a ten-minute short. If she hadn't already been in the habit of paying attention to her dreams, she would never have created the film.

Filmmaker James Cameron "was fighting a 102-degree fever when a vision of a robot dragging itself along the floor with a knife came to him in his sleep," writes Stacy Conradt in an article on MentalFloss.com. That dream became the inspiration for his film *The Terminator*.

## HEALTH AND NUTRITION

As I was writing this section, the 2016 holiday season had just wrapped up. During the week prior, we had a house full of kids and enough desserts to send a small village into a diabetic coma. My dad informed me that we had gone through four industrial-size bags of cheese and one hundred tortillas in just a few days. Meanwhile, my creative output came to a halt. By New Year's Day, my body was basically saying, "Please stop doing this to me." That night I ate a salad for dinner and went to sleep by nine p.m. This section, which I had been struggling with, finally started to come together.

Gene Bowman, head of nutrition and brain health at the Nestlé Institute of Health Sciences, published the results of a study in *Neurology* that confirmed why a good night's sleep and healthy dinner could lead to a creative breakthrough. The study, "Nutrient Biomarker Patterns, Cognitive Function, and MRI Measures of Brain Aging," showed that people whose diets were high in B vitamins and omega-3 fatty acids had higher scores on cognitive tests than people with lower levels of both. People with diets that were high in trans fats had poorer cognitive performance as revealed in thinking and memory tests. As your parents probably told you, "Take your vitamins and don't eat junk food."

If there's one thing that became apparent after my conversation with food blogger and neuroscientist Darya Pino Rose, it's that nutrition is not a one-size-fits-all solution and affects all of us differently. "Science is great at telling us what works on a population level, but it's shitty at telling you what works for you," says Rose. In spite of all the excitement around fitness blogs, biohacking, and the latest diet fad (Paleo, Ketogenic, Bulletproof, etc.), you have to learn to listen to *your* body. You will have to experiment and develop a deeper awareness of how your food affects you mentally and creatively.

Despite our differences, we do have some commonalities when it comes to the link between nutrition and cognitive capabilities.

## BLOOD SUGAR

"Blood sugar is such a big factor in how you feel. It's a big factor in your mood and your ability to think clearly, and that's true no matter what. There might be people who can process a sugary meal better than others, but regardless, if it's processed poorly everybody is going to feel the negative effects," says Rose. She adds, "Your blood sugar levels have a massive impact on how your brain works."

The solution to regulating our blood sugar is to eat more unprocessed foods. Basically anything that comes in a jar or box is likely off the list. Blogger and author James Clear has a simple approach of sticking to the outside aisles of the grocery store, which is where all the real foods tend to be stocked. "One of the main things that people notice when eating unprocessed food is that they have more energy and can think more clearly," says Rose.

But don't just blindly follow the advice of anyone, including me. Find what type of food intake makes *you* more focused and creative. To find out what nutrition is right for you, try this: Make a list of what you eat each day for a week. For that same week, keep a record of your creative efforts. Then make note of the days on which you were at your peak creatively, and see what foods played a role. More than anything else this is about cultivating awareness.

While a deep dive into nutrition is beyond the scope of this book, what's most important is a simple mantra from the world of computer science: garbage in, garbage out. If you put garbage into your body, it's likely that's what will come out in terms of your creative output.

## EXERCISE AND PHYSICAL FITNESS

Exercise is another one of those not-so-obvious hacks for creativity. It provides us with both physical and cognitive benefits, and as a bonus helps us sleep better—a lot of bang for your creative buck.

"Exercise increases the creation of mitochondria—the cellular structures that generate and maintain our energy—both in our muscles and in our brain, which may explain the mental edge we often experience after a workout. Studies also show that getting the heart rate up enhances neurogenesis—the ability to grow new brain cells—in adults," says David Jacobs, a professor in the division of epidemiology and community health at the School of Public Health at the University of Minnesota, in an article on the *Scientific American* website.

For a study published in *Neurology* titled "Cardiorespiratory Fitness and Cognitive Function in Middle Age," Jacobs and his colleagues followed 2,747 adults between the ages of eighteen and thirty for twenty-five years. Physical fitness of the participants was evaluated in 1985 using a treadmill test in which they walked up an incline that became increasingly steeper for ten minutes. The lowest performers lasted for seven minutes whereas high performers lasted for thirteen. A second test was conducted in 2005 that revealed that those who were in better shape in 1985 were also more likely to be fit twenty years later. Five years later, in 2010, participants were exposed to a number of cognitive tests "assessing memory, processing speed and executive function—measures of our abilities to learn, reason and problem solve." Those who had been physically fit in 1985 performed *10 percent better on the tests compared to their less fit counterparts.*

When I asked graffiti artist and author Erik Wahl about how he prepares for a speaking engagement, he said, "I treat it as if I'm an athlete training for a game." As creators we're like athletes, and our art is our game. Almost all the creators I know have an exercise routine that seems to fuel their creative work. AJ Leon, Reema Zaman, Haruki Murakami, and many others are runners. Brian Ferguson, the cofounder of a virtual reality start-up that films medical surgeries, is an avid skier and surfer. Professional guitarist and Unmistakable Creative guest Joe Goodkin is also a marathon runner.

Physical movement can even deepen the creative process. Choreographer Twyla Tharp begins her days going to the gym and says that "in a state of physical warmth, dancers touch their moments of greatest physical potential." Warmth, she says, enables them to "trust their bodies" and "that's where the magic happens." Given that "dance is all about physical movement and

LISTEN TO: **MOLLY PEACOCK**

Great technique means that you have to abandon perfectionism. Perfectionism either stops you cold or slows you down too much. Yet, paradoxically, it's proficiency that allows a person to make any art at all; you must have technical skill to accomplish anything, but you also must have passion, which, in an odd way, is technique forgotten. The joy of technique is the bulging bag of tricks it gives you to solve your dilemmas. Craft gives you the tools for reparation. And teachers give you craft, for a good teacher urges you beyond your childish perfectionism. From there you proceed into the practice that eventually becomes expertise.

exertion," starting the day at the gym enables her to perform at her best when she enters the dance studio.

I never truly made strides as a writer until I became a surfer. I've done both for roughly the same amount of time. My most significant creative breakthroughs always occur after a good surf session or a day on the mountain snowboarding. The flow from my physical activities ripples into my creative efforts.

Deep immersion in a physical activity allows the mind to quiet, and at the same time allows us to hear our truest voice and connect with our heart's deepest desire. We may not hear it in the moment, but we certainly will afterward. The most intense physical activities can take us into a place of solitude that can't possibly be accessed by sitting in a room in silence. Taking physical risks equips us with an ability to take creative leaps. One friend, who composed ad jingles, had always considered herself a "jogger" and ran two miles a day, no more, no less, for years. When she challenged herself to run a 10K race, she came in next to last. But in the exhilaration of racing, she had an epiphany. If she could finish a 10K, she could tackle an opera.

Listening to yourself is about hearing your unmistakable voice. "You will never develop an authentic voice unless you are fully aware of what makes you unique and pursue it boldly," says Accidental Creative founder Todd Henry. Often what makes each of us unique is muffled beneath the masks we wear, the labels we identify with, and the stories we tell ourselves. As we cultivate the practices in this section, what starts to emerge is the through-line of our work and the fullest expression of who we are. It's from here that our most resonant, impactful, and fulfilling work will emerge.

# UNMISTAKABLE PRACTICE:
## ACTIVITIES AND EXERCISES

### WHAT WOULD HAPPEN IF . . .

Fill a page of your journal with your most ambitious and audacious ideas with no concern for how they will come to fruition. Then write down a list of questions. For example, here are some questions along with my own answers to get you started.

**What advice would I give my younger self?**

*You're sitting in a business class, dreaming of climbing the corporate ladder. What will come as a surprise is the aversion you will have to that idea in about ten years. Life won't go according to plan. In some ways it will be far better than anything you can currently imagine. You'll write books, start a company, speak to audiences of thousands, and travel the world. Getting there won't be easy. You'll go through peaks and valleys, but the experience will ultimately turn you into who you are destined to be. You'll also be shocked to learn that despite your athletic ineptitude you'll become an avid surfer and snowboarder. So I'd tell you not to worry, but I know that advice will fall on deaf ears. By the time you're thirty-nine your priorities will have changed, and you'll have realized that there's an infinite value that can't be measured when you find meaning and purpose in your work.*

**What would the most ideal version of my life look like?**

*In my most ideal life, I live in North County San Diego, where I surf almost every day and do yoga multiple times a week. I speak, write, and run a highly profitable media company. I'm in a wonderful relationship with an amazing woman who is creative, athletic, and adventurous. We travel multiple times a year to surf and snowboard. My work gives me an opportunity to express myself creatively every day.*

**What's one life lesson I've learned for every year of my life?**

*My personal birthday writing tradition, here is my thirty-eighth birthday list:*

1. Write every day.

2. If it matters, put it on your calendar.

3. Have a reason to get up in the morning.

4. Read more books and less online.

5. Almost all change begins with changing habits.

6. Keep moving forward.

7. Check the alignment of your compass.

8. Draw a line in the sand. Decide who your art is for and who it's not for.

9. Keep exploring, keep learning, and keep growing.

10. I've become the antithesis of what my destiny would dictate.

11. Dare greatly, fall down, and get back up.

12. Pay it forward.

13. Straight and narrow paths rarely intersect with interesting destinations.

14. You really can only connect the dots looking back.

15. Don't waste too much time on the internet.

16. Find three books that you return to at least once a month.

17. You can improve with age.

18. Pure work can't be done when you're trying to prove people wrong.

19. Always carry a notebook/take notes.

20. Ditch the checklist of dreams you pretend not to have.

21. If you don't care about what you do, it will only take you so far.

22. Don't live according to a deferred life plan.

23. Your work has to be about something greater than yourself.

24. Don't compromise values and standards for short-term profit.

25. Sometimes you get what you want by giving up the desire for it.

26. Freaking out doesn't alter the outcome of anything.

27. Don't worry too much about the future. Don't dwell too much on the past.

28. Give it a little bit more time before you quit.

29. Don't be afraid to pull the plug.

30. One word can change your life.

31. Come up with your own definition of happiness.

32. Quality trumps quantity when it comes to friends.

33. People are in our lives for a reason, a season, or a lifetime.

34. Ride waves, mountains—do something that involves a board under your feet.

35. If you're going to challenge the status quo, you will be misunderstood.

36. Celebrate small wins.

37. Value your time.

38. If you live in San Francisco, read street signs carefully. (They should erect a statue in my honor with the amount of money I've spent on parking tickets there.)

**How do I want the world to be better/different for my having been here?**

○ More people are working jobs they love.

○ More people are expressing their creativity.

○ Education has been reformed to not be a one-size-fits-all solution.

Each day for the next week, use your journal to explore your answers to these questions.

## LISTEN TO YOUR DREAMS

Learning to listen to your dreams can be one of the most fruitful parts of your creative practice. The first step, of course, is to learn how to recall your dreams. Some people seem to remember every detail, while others—like me—have to make a conscious effort to tap the sleeping brain.

To begin, simply set an intention. Tell yourself you want to remember your dreams tonight. When you wake up, whether it's in the middle of the night or in the morning, before you move, open your eyes, or do anything, try to summon your dreams. You might recall an image, a word, a feeling—just keep focusing on whatever you receive. Once you think you've remembered as much as you can, write it down in a notebook you've put next to your bed. (They make handy dream pens that light up so you can read what you wrote.) If you're more visual, sketch what you can remember. Avoid using any alarm system, which interrupts your dream access.

Start doing this every night, but now add reading what you've written each evening before bedtime to your practice. Remind yourself that you *will* remember your dreams. After a week or so, you should be recalling more and more of your sleeping mind's creativity.

## YOUR CREATIVE CHILD

Think about when you were seven years old: When were you happiest? What were you doing? If you weren't in school, where were you most likely to be found? What was the feeling you had?

When my father gave me a Sony Walkman, he planted the seed for a love of music that would show up over and over in my life.

- I started playing the tuba in seventh grade.

- I assembled a slide show for the Indian student club at Berkeley. The soundtrack got more of my attention than all the other details.

- For my first conference, I had a song for every speaker and a soundtrack for the entire event.

The sound of music has been a constant creative presence in my life and one of the sources of my joy.

When we look back and take inventory, we'll start to uncover how creativity shows up in our lives early and often, and how its presence is always there, even if we're not consciously aware of it. Listening to your young self reminds you what direction your creativity most easily flowed. It's a great clue to your most effortless efforts.

## CREATIVE AUTOBIOGRAPHY

Beginning with your childhood again, list every creative activity you can remember. Go right up to the present. Include both large and small examples. Here is my list:

### Kindergarten

- Sewing a doll

- Building things out of blocks

- Made a paper plate man with construction paper as legs (which I chased around in a blizzard)

### First Grade/Second Grade

- School plays

- Christmas crafts and ornaments

### Fourth Grade

○ Narrated *Mary Poppins* school play

### Fifth Grade

○ Attempted the world's longest division problem and tried to get into *The Guinness Book of World Records*

### Sixth Grade

○ Started playing the trombone

### Seventh Grade

○ Pretended to be a journalist reporting crimes, and recorded a video in which I turned all of my classmates into the criminals

○ Started playing the tuba

### Eighth Grade/Ninth Grade

○ Started a candy business that was shut down by the choir teacher

○ Mainly being in the band and playing tuba

### Tenth Grade/Eleventh Grade

○ Started writing short stories

### In College/Twenties

○ A slide show set to music for the Indian student club

○ An exposé about the start-up from hell

○ A Bollywood parody music video with my roommate

### In My Thirties

○ Multiple blogs

○ The podcast

○ Books

○ The Instigator Experience conference

○ Animated series

Refer to this list whenever you hear yourself saying, "I'm not very creative."

## CREATIVE GENOGRAM

If you're still wondering or doubting whether you're even creative, try this: Ask your family to help you record as many relatives as possible, maybe the last three or four generations. Note the ways in which each person was creative, including knitting, cooking, flower arranging, and party planning, as well as the more traditional arts such as painting, music, dance, and so forth.

We all come from a long lineage of artists and creators, whether we realize it or not.

## CREATIVE FAMILY TREE

My own creative genealogy consists of cooks, visual artists, photographers, dancers, writers, and musicians.

○ My mother and grandmother are known in our family for their colorful meals and diverse repertoire of both South and North Indian cuisine in their kitchen. Even though we're South Indian, my mother often jokes that there must have been a mix-up in the hospital because I was born in New Delhi and for the most part hate South Indian food.

○ My grandmother's oldest sister did Rangoli, a colorful design made on the floor near the entrance to a house to welcome guests.

○ When she was in college at Berkeley, my sister worked as a hostess in a French café where she developed a love for baking, which became her creative and therapeutic outlet. In her residency interviews, she was most frequently asked about that job and asked to teach her colleagues how to make desserts.

○ My paternal grandfather, even after his retirement, was always writing letters and papers that he submitted to scientific journals.

○ Throughout our childhood, my father took thousands of pictures of our family and of our travels. His photography will be his creative legacy.

○ Two of my cousins are both visual artists and hobbyist fashion designers, outside of their jobs as engineers.

○ My cousin Srish plays two Indian instruments: the tabla and veena.

# PART THREE

# LISTENING TO YOUR ENVIRONMENT

n the summer of 2014, I moved temporarily to a house in Carlsbad, California, that my friend Matt Monroe described as "a middle-aged youth hostel with none of the benefits of a youth hostel." Roommates never interacted with one another. The landlord did nothing to maintain the landscaping. The kitchen had an ongoing ant problem and my bedroom felt a bit like a prison cell. I went through some of my darkest times while I lived there. I avoided spending time at "home" as much as possible.

More than anything, living in that house made me realize the profound impact of environment on our lives, our work, and our creativity. "Everything you see, smell, taste, touch, and hear is an environment. That environment is either adding energy or draining energy. It's either inspiring you or expiring you," said the Ultimate Game of Life founder Jim Bunch on an episode of *The Unmistakable Creative.* My environment was draining my energy and my bank account at the same time. It was so toxic for my creativity that I gave my notice and moved back into my parents' house.

It might seem counterintuitive, but my parents' house was much more conducive to creativity. It was clean and a meal was always on the table. My parents let me convert a downstairs bedroom into my home office. When I told a friend that if I had a million-dollar recording studio, I'd hang framed prints of our guests on my wall, she said, "What's stopping you?" The answer was nothing. I hung up framed prints of former Unmistakable Creative guests whom I looked up to and found inspiring. This is an example of designing an environment that supports creativity.

Soon after I moved in with my parents, I read a life-changing book that happens to be called *The Life-Changing Magic of Tidying Up*. Author Marie Kondo uses the question "Does this spark joy?" to determine what you should keep and what you should get rid of. By asking myself "Does this spark joy?" I learned to listen to my environment in a dramatically new way. I started with my bookshelf. After putting all the books that I didn't like in a box, the majority of the remaining books were published by Penguin. The unexpected and synchronistic result? I received a note from a Penguin editor expressing interest in publishing my book. Eventually, I threw away every piece of clothing that I had worn during one of the worst years of my life. The next things to go were fractured friendships that I still had ties to on Facebook.

Listening to your environment allows you to remove what

doesn't matter and make space for what does. By designing environments that add energy and increase your focus, you make room for more creative work.

Despite my not really wanting to move home, it turned out to be a perfect environment in which to write a book. By January of the following year, I'd submitted my first manuscript, our business was profitable again, and I had regained my confidence. A positive environment can be that powerful .

Today I'm fanatical about environments because I'm so aware of their impact.

Our environments are always communicating with us through the way they make us feel. By paying attention to how we feel, we learn to listen to our environments. The first thing that probably comes to mind for you thinking about environment is your physical space. But environment is much broader than that. It includes the people you associate with, the information you consume, your spiritual beliefs, your physical body, and much more.

## YOUR PHYSICAL SPACE

Where you create might be a room, a shared studio, a library, or a boat—what matters is making it sing to you.

When we clear physical clutter, we make mental space. "Messy surroundings and an untidy life reflect a weakened metaphysical and psychological state. . . . Order helps you feel confident," says author Stuart Wilde.

Before I go to sleep, I make sure that there's nothing on my desk other than the pen I want to write with in the morning and a Moleskine notebook. If there's anything on the floor or any clutter in the room, I make a point to remove it, and I make my bed the moment I wake up in the morning. To me, a clean space equals a clear mind.

Think about how you feel when you get into your car right after a car wash or step into your home after it's been cleaned. You might feel calm, focused, clear, and inspired.

Now imagine if you felt like that all the time in all your physical spaces, especially your creative work areas. The spaces in which we create are sanctuaries and should be treated as such.

*Minimalism: A Documentary About the Important Things,* with Joshua Fields Millburn and Ryan Nicodemus, is a perfect example of the impact that our physical space has on our lives. Throughout the film, as people rid their lives of unnecessary possessions, they find themselves living lives of greater meaning, significance, and purpose.

One person in particular who stood out was Courtney Carver. Shortly after getting married, she was diagnosed with MS. By getting rid of excess and material possessions, she's not only had no relapses, but is in better health than before she was diagnosed. On her blog, *Be More with Less,* Carver started Project 333, which invites you to dress with thirty-three items or fewer for three months, which turned into a movement to live with less. When you minimize the number of possessions you have, you increase the likelihood that you absolutely love what you have, and that what you wear is part of an environment that inspires you.

## CREATING YOUR BEST SPACE

The space in which you create should reflect not only who you are, but who you aspire to become. Consider lighting, furniture, wall color, smells, and feng shui: Are these elements sparking joy? Then try some of the hacks below. I think you'll be surprised by the effect they have on your creativity and productivity.

### Get rid of anything you don't love

Marie Kondo's "Does this spark joy?" filter is a very effective way to determine what you should get rid of and what you should keep. When it comes to adding anything to your space, my friend Charmaine Haworth, a speaker, coach, and healer, has a simple rule: "If you don't absolutely love it, don't buy it." Every object in our physical space has associated memories and emotions, from the clothes we wear, to the pen we write with, to the car we drive. If the emotions and memories you have associated with something in your physical space are negative, consider getting rid of those possessions.

When I moved into a new apartment, I took this approach to my bedsheets, bookshelves, and nightstands. Every day when I wake up, the space feels calm, soothing, and inspiring. Fall in love with your creative space.

### Clear out as much clutter as possible

We often hang on to boxes that our electronics came in, junk mail, and much more. One of my favorite clutter-clearing tools is called the Perch Urbio. You mount a magnetic plate to a flat surface and add cup holders, mail slots, and more that attach via a magnet. I have one on the back of my bedroom door, and this ensures that there's absolutely no clutter on my desk when I wake up in the morning.

### Environment math

I've read this advice everywhere from blogs to books; it's an easy, effective rule of thumb. For each item you bring into your home, whether it's a new shirt, a pillow, or a magazine, discard something comparable. If you keep up this habit, you'll never become overwhelmed by stuff and your creativity will have psychic and physical space to flourish.

### Give everything a designated space

Have you ever spent twenty minutes looking for your keys only to discover that they were in the pockets of the pants you wore yesterday? By the time you find them, you're usually flustered and you find it hard to focus on anything. "Having systems like key hooks, cell phone trays, and a special hook or drawer for sunglasses externalizes the effort so that we don't have to keep everything in our heads," says Daniel Levitin, author of *The Organized Mind*.

## *Visual reminders*

By filling your physical environment with visual reminders of your most important goals, what matters most to you, and what inspires you, you'll increase the likelihood of reaching those goals. Additionally, consider filling the space with reminders of concepts that have a profound impact on your thinking. For example, after reading *The Four Agreements* by Don Miguel Ruiz, I wanted a daily reminder of the ideas. So I ordered a poster, had it framed, and hung it on my wall.

## *Power questions*

On my desk I have a spiral-bound set of three-by-five cards. Each card has a question on it. The first thing I see when I sit down to work in the morning are what life coach Tony Robbins refers to as power questions. "Your brain will give you any answer to any question you ask it," he says. By starting the day with questions, you prime the brain. The beauty of power questions is that your brain will come up with answers to your questions even if they don't seem to make logical sense yet.

**Here are my examples:**

1. What's great about my life?
   *I love my job, live two minutes from the water, get to surf every day, and work with an amazing team.*

2. What am I most happy about right now?

   *It's 80 degrees and sunny outside (the answer to this question is different every day).*

3. What am I most proud of in our business?

   *I'm proud of how far we've come since almost going out of business in 2014.*

By asking these questions every morning, your brain will eventually link the positive emotion created by the answers to waking up in the morning. This results in what is known as an anchor. Just as Ivan Pavlov used the sound of a bell to make his dogs salivate, we can use our questions to prime our brains for a positive state of mind.

## TOLERATIONS

Your physical space isn't limited to just the setup of a room or desk. It includes any physical object that you come in contact with (e.g., clothes you wear, devices you use, dishes in your kitchen, etc.).

Often we have *tolerations* in our physical space, items that are in less than optimal condition. Tolerations might include cracked screens on phones, clothes with holes or stains, and scratches or dents on cars. We *tolerate* such concrete objects for a long time and we pay a price.

Tolerations might seem like minor inconveniences. But when

you remove them from your life, you'll find that other areas of your life are positively affected. "You can't change one environment and not have it affect the others. If you upgrade one environment, it will send a ripple through the others," says Jim Bunch. Removing tolerations is one of the easiest environmental upgrades you can make.

Recently, I traded in my old car for a new one. The moment I drove the new car off the lot, I felt as if the weight of the world had been lifted off my shoulders. Reflecting on it, I realized that almost everything I had subconsciously associated with my previous car were painful memories from one of the most difficult years of my life. Tolerations can weigh that heavily on us without our even realizing it.

In the midst of writing this book, the Ikea chair from which I'd recorded hundreds of interviews and written my previous book started to fall apart. When the new chair arrived, I was stunned at the level of discomfort I'd been tolerating for more than a year.

Try making a list of all the tolerations in your life. For example:

- Charger cables that don't work

- Torn or worn-out clothing

- Devices with one or two broken functions

- Jerry-rigged kitchen appliances

- Furniture that is in poor condition (desks, chairs, bookshelves, etc.)

After you've identified them, eliminate one. If you're able to eliminate one a week, you'll notice a significant shift in your focus, clarity, and creativity.

## YOUR NATURAL SPACE

For the longest time I thought immersing yourself in nature was reserved for granola hippies who shopped at REI and wore Birkenstocks. Yet two of my major activities, surfing and snowboarding, are more than physical exercise; they provide an opportunity to benefit from spending time in the natural world. The ocean, in particular, has been one of my greatest teachers and the source of many of my creative ideas.

The ocean has taught me to endure adversity, to take wave after wave on the head so that I might catch one. It's taught me to be patient, because sometimes you wait twenty minutes between waves, living in the moment and keeping your eyes on the horizon. It's taught me to accept failure and get back up after I fall. It's taught me to see the world as a more abundant place because there's always another wave coming. All of these lessons are invaluable for a creative practice.

As a surfer, I always say that all it takes is one good wave to make a surf session. That one wave keeps you coming back for more. If I caught one good wave, it was worth the hassle of putting on a wetsuit and taking a few waves on the head in order to catch one.

It's the same with creative practice—one good sentence, one

brushstroke, one verse, one shot through the lens of a camera, one move on the dance floor—that's all it really takes to keep you coming back for more.

It turns out I'm not alone.

Nature has been the source of creative inspiration for artists, poets, philosophers, innovators, and entrepreneurs throughout history. Mark Zuckerberg is famous for taking long walks (as was Steve Jobs before him). Kary Mullis came up with his Nobel Prize–winning discovery of the polymerase chain reaction by thinking about his research while surfing.

LISTEN TO: **TAMI LYNN KENT**

**Creativity begins with an impulse, but it is practice that hones the form. Having a creative practice makes the time, space, and energy—a routine over time—that is necessary to formulate a creation. Making creativity a routine practice can assist you in overcoming resistance to your creative impulses. Rather than becoming bogged down in trying to create something specific or achieve a certain outcome, simply begin the practice and engage the energy that arrives. Take the photo, write the sentence, move the body, sing the note, press the piano key, moisten the paintbrush, plant the seed; begin.**

In her book *The Nature Fix*, Florence Williams set out to uncover the impact that nature has on our happiness, health, and creativity. She cites the Japanese practice of *shinrin-yoku* (aka forest bathing) and notes that taking a walk through the forest has been shown to reduce cortisol levels by 12 percent. "When people walk in nature, they obsess over negative thoughts much less than when they walk in a city," says Williams.

Our time in nature can be awe-inspiring. Williams adds, "When they are vast, nature scenes and events can connect us to deeper forces in the world. At the very least, these types of experiences appear to alter us temporarily." It's from these deeper forces that creative ideas are often born. A state of awe "promotes curiosity" and allows us to "experience things out of our normal frame of reference." In my own experience, being outside of the normal frame of reference (i.e., sitting in front of a computer) allows me to see what I couldn't see before and, most important, to listen to my creative voice in a way that I couldn't before. Nature is powerful fuel for our creative fire.

Nature allows us to tap into the power of what Harvard neuroscientist Dr. Srinivasan Pillay describes as the "power of the unfocused mind." We're able to let go of rational, logical, and linear thought patterns. The ideas that have been percolating in the unconscious rise to the surface of our minds. In many of his conversations with clients and patients who have sold their companies, Pillay found that the core of the ideas that led to their success occurred when they tapped into the unfocused mind.

When children with symptoms of ADHD spent time outdoors, they experienced higher levels of focus. As somebody who was diagnosed with ADHD as an adult, I can attest to the role that nature has played in my own ability to focus. When I sit down to work after a good surf session, my productivity skyrockets. Countless seeds of creative ideas have come to me after dropping into a wave. Paradoxically, not actively thinking about the problem that I was trying to solve led to the solution.

Our time in nature serves as a sort of mental reboot. It drastically reduces or shuts off the flow of information to our mind and turns up the volume on our creative voices. Immersion in nature results in focus, flow, and creative breakthroughs. Whether it's in woods, an ocean, gardens, streets, terraces, parks, lakes, or streams, spending time outdoors is an invaluable element of any creative practice.

If you aren't ready for complete immersion in nature, take baby steps. Get outside and take a short walk. Stroll around a garden, sit under a tree, gaze at a river. You'll find that even a few minutes spent with the natural world can reset and fuel your creativity.

## YOUR SOUND ENVIRONMENT

Most of us think of music first when we consider our aural environment. But we receive many other kinds of aural input, from subways roaring below an apartment to neighbors laughing to an overactive refrigerator. Or consider all the sounds of nature: wind, rain, thunder, birds, crickets. Now think about how to take control of any sounds you hear, whether calming or stimulating, soothing or irritating.

Let's start with music!

Music can influence our productivity and creativity like a direct shot to the brain—literally. "When listening to music, brainwaves move from the high-beta of normal waking consciousness down into the meditative (and trance-inducing) range of alpha and theta. At the same time, levels of stress hormones like nor-epinephrine and cortisol drop, while social bonding and reward chemicals like dopamine, endorphins, serotonin, and oxytocin spike," write authors Steven Kotler and Jamie Wheal in their book *Stealing Fire*.

A number of music apps affect our brainwaves. Apps like the online radio service Pandora now offer a "concentration" station. My preferred choice is Focus@Will. The app helps to put your brain in a focused state while you're working. It filters out the noise in your environment and increases your level of concentration. I use the app while I'm reading and writing. The last few paragraphs you've read have all been written "under the influence" of Focus@Will.

Whether you choose to listen to music with or without lyrics depends on the complexity and nature of the task. Writing or reading would be challenging while listening to music with lyrics because both require verbal processing. If you're painting or sculpting, you can listen to music with lyrics, podcasts, or even audiobooks because what you're doing does not require verbal processing.

- My friend Angela England, creator of the website Untrained Housewife, echoed these sentiments when I asked her about her creative practice: "If it's rhythmic and repetitive I listen to podcasts. If I need to think in words, I use music instead."

- Another friend, a ceramicist, listens to the same Philip Glass piece over and over again while she works.

- My roommate, Michael Ernst, a graphic designer and visual artist, listens to classical music early in the day and a wide variety of music later in the day.

- Authors Ryan Holiday and Steven Kotler listen to the same track (usually techno music without lyrics) on repeat.

## AMBIENT NOISE

A study in the *Journal of Consumer Research*, titled "Is Noise Always Bad? Exploring the Effects of Ambient Noise on Creative Cognition," found that "while a moderate level of noise produces just enough distraction to induce disfluency, leading to higher creativity, a very high level of noise induces too much distraction so as to actually reduce the amount of processing, leading to lower creativity." To put it more simply, just the right amount of noise might have a positive effect on our creativity. But too much noise and we'll be very distracted from the task at hand.

A moderate level of noise would be the buzz of a coffee shop or a white noise machine. A loud bar in which you're having to shout out your order or can barely hear yourself think will be too much. If you find that the background noise hinders rather than helps your focus, it's too loud.

## THIS IS YOUR BRAIN ON WATER

In an episode of *The Unmistakable Creative*, wild water advocate and entrepreneurial marine biologist Wallace Nichols described the impact of water on the brain. When we are looking at a body of water, the view is relatively simple. "Auditorily our world is simplified and the default mode network is activated, which is a more contemplative, self-referential perspective," said Nichols. To experience these benefits you don't have to be physically at the edge of water or get into it (although you're missing out on one of the great joys of life if you don't). By listening to the *sounds* of rain, waterfalls, or a stream, you can tap into the creative and cognitive benefits of water.

Even something as simple as sitting near a fountain or taking a fifteen-minute shower can produce the same effect in your own work. When I hear the sounds of waves crashing onshore, it takes me back to some of my fondest memories and puts me in an incredibly calm and contemplative state in which many of my creative breakthroughs tend to occur.

## NOISE CANCELLATION HEADPHONES

One of the most important investments I've ever made in my creative practice was a pair of high-quality noise cancellation headphones. We often don't realize just how distracting noise of any kind can be until we've deliberately drowned it out. Environmental noise is like a low-level virus: You don't realize how much it's sapping your energy until it's gone. When you go out of your way to block out noise, you'll find that your ability to focus for an extended period of time increases. Whether you're working from home, in a coffee shop, or on an airplane, a pair of good headphones will give you a significant return on your investment in terms of productivity and creative output. I even know a novelist who is able to write on the New York City subway by wearing high-end headphones. An added bonus: When I wear headphones (I recommend Bose) on flights, I land feeling much less tired than otherwise, even on transcontinental trips.

## YOUR TECH ENVIRONMENT

You have to deliberately design what *does* become part of your digital—or memetic—environment. In other words, you have to choose the books you read, the podcasts you listen to, and the shows you watch with care.

The paradox of technology is that the very tools that facilitate our creativity also inhibit it. How we approach and resolve that paradox is essential to our creativity. When our use of technology is not mindful and deliberate, we become its slave rather than its master. And this gradually erodes our creative capacities, attention spans, and the depth needed to create work of consequence and significance.

Tools should supplement our efforts, not replace them. We don't want the camera's lens to replace a photographer's eye. We don't want the mixing board to replace the musician's instrument. When our tools replace our efforts rather than supplement them, and what we make is measured in efficiency as opposed to originality, we turn from creatives into cogs.

Don't get me wrong, I'm not a Luddite or the next Unabomber. I love the internet and technology. The internet has made it possible for me to write my books, record my podcasts, and share them with the world. But I try hard to be deliberate in how I deploy such tools. For many people, it's quite the opposite. Their use of apps, tools, and technology is habitual. They never change the default settings on the apps they download or the websites they visit. Their behavior becomes unconscious, reactive, and controlled by technology. And rather than supporting their creativity, their use of technology gets in the way of it.

To develop a more mindful relationship with technology, it helps to understand how it affects our behavior.

## DOPAMINE AND DISTRACTIONS

Two essential traits we need to sustain high-value creative output today are:

The ability to focus on something that is demanding of our attention for an extended period of time

The ability to remain present while we're working

In order to battle hundreds of daily sources of distraction that sabotage both these abilities, we have to understand how technology affects us from a neurological perspective.

Nearly every source of distraction has one culprit: dopamine. Dopamine is the brain's pleasure chemical, a neurotransmitter that is released when we receive an email, a Facebook "like," a social network notification, or a text message. It's the same chemical that is activated by cocaine. It plays a major role in all of our digital habits, and, like cocaine, it's extremely addictive.

Perhaps the most insidious thing about dopamine is that it provides us with a sense of satisfaction that doesn't last. Dopamine is not only hijacking our ability to focus and be present, but slowly damaging both. This is why when we check email, Twitter, or Facebook first thing in the morning, we're likely to find ourselves checking them all day long—we want that rush again and again.

## THE HABIT-FORMING DESIGN OF APPS AND PRODUCTS

Most of the technology that we deal with on a daily basis is intentionally designed to be habit forming:

- Facebook is designed to keep you checking Facebook.

- Instagram is designed to keep you taking pictures and looking at other people's pictures.

- Google is designed to keep you searching.

These companies want you to be not only a registered user, but a customer who has a daily habit of using their products. Why? Because the more you use their products, the more money they make.

Each of these companies provides us with variable rewards. The fact that you never know what you're going to get, or what you'll find when you log in, keeps you coming back for more.

Now that you have an overview of how many of today's digital distractions are designed to be habit forming, ask yourself the question that *Deep Work* author Cal Newport posed to me:

> Is this one of the small number of things that's adding a significant amount of value to my life?

New apps and new websites that "everybody needs to be on" are continuously popping up. While the so-called social media gurus and internet celebrities sing the praises of distracting technology, don't forget that many have a strong financial incentive to push their use.

Just now a message from *Medium* popped up telling me about the sixty-two—sixty-two!—websites that will make me "incredibly smarter." I don't have time to be that smart if I want to be creative. Many of these products stand squarely in the way of being able not only to listen to creativity, but to actually hear it.

## THIS IS YOUR BRAIN ON THE INTERNET

It's clear that the internet is inextricably woven into our lives. *Wired* magazine founding editor Kevin Kelly has gone so far as to say that the internet is "a low level constant presence like electricity: always around us, always on, and subterranean." Obviously, then, we need to know exactly how the internet affects our brains and what impact that has on our creativity.

Jocelyn Glei, author of *Unsubscribe: How to Kill Email Anxiety, Avoid Distractions, and Get Real Work Done*, described our addiction in an interview on *The Unmistakable Creative*:

> Your email functions like a slot machine. Most of the time you pull the lever and you lose. But then every once in a while you get an email from a long-lost childhood friend or an invitation to speak at a conference that's very flattering. So these random rewards are mixed in with all that annoying stuff, and mixed in with all the junk that activates this seeking mechanism in our brain and makes us want to go back and check again and again to see if there are any of those random rewards in our inboxes. That's part of the driving force behind that addiction.

This addiction does far more than decrease our productivity and reduce the likelihood of creative breakthroughs. It does long-term damage to our ability to focus and be present. It turns us into what Cal Newport refers to as "the cognitive equivalent of being an athlete who smokes." Our harmless "checks" while waiting in line at the grocery store or boarding a flight are not as harmless as we might imagine. If we're constantly giving in to digital distractions, mindlessly shifting our attention from app to app and website to website, this creates what is known as an attention residue, which "reduces cognitive performance for a non-trivial [amount of] time to follow."

What we do *before* we do creative work has just as much of an impact as how we work. When we've spent hours letting our attention drift from one external stimulus to another, we'll have a much more challenging time managing our attention when we want to work. This is why we must be able to resist our temptation to give in to distractions even when we are not doing creative work.

LISTEN TO: JIM BUNCH

**Everything that you see, hear, smell, taste, and touch is an environment. Those environments are either adding energy or draining energy. They are either increasing your focus or decreasing your focus.**

According to Nicholas Carr, author of *The Shallows: What the Internet Is Doing to Our Brains,* when we are online, we "willingly accept the loss of concentration and focus, the division of our attention and the fragmentation of our thoughts, in return for the wealth of compelling or at least diverting information we receive." In other words we're accepting the loss of two vital attributes for consistent creative output: focus and attention. When we're on the internet, our attention continually shifts from one stimulus to another, and we do great harm to our ability to focus on anything for an extended period of time. Sadly, "the more we use the Web, the more we train our brain to be distracted—to process information very quickly and very efficiently but without sustained attention," says Carr.

*The Shallows* was originally published in 2010, and in those few years since, the internet and other sources of distraction have played an even greater role in our lives. Almost everyone has a smartphone and uses at least one social media platform, if not several. But the price of being perpetually connected is a lack of progress on meaningful creative work, a lack of presence, and the loss of time spent on activities that improve our lives, like reading great books, writing, making art, and having deep and meaningful conversations with the people in our lives.

A few months ago, I was visiting with an old friend from college, who seemed anxious and restless. He'd gotten into the habit of checking his email so many times a day that he'd lost count. If he hadn't received any new messages, he'd reread the emails he'd sent to other people. This seemingly harmless habit had a not so harmless by-product. Even though he had been an avid reader, he now had a difficult time reading for more than five minutes.

As research for this section of the book, I decided to take a five-day sabbatical from social media. That meant no taking pictures for Instagram, no posting or logging in to Facebook, and no using Twitter. It helped that I was in the mountains of Colorado snowboarding. On the first day, I noticed an immediate change. Words started to flow when I sat down to write. My anxiety dissipated. World War III did not break out in my inbox. I slept better.

When I returned from snowboarding, I received a text from my business partner, Brian Koehn, letting me know that we had landed another sponsor. One of my biggest worries while I was constantly checking my email (the loss of sponsors for our podcast) evaporated. And this was only the first day of my social media hiatus!

While a day on the mountain snowboarding or in the water surfing might seem frivolous, it often provides the necessary disconnect we need, not only to listen to our creativity, but to hear what it is telling us.

## ELIMINATING AND MANAGING DISTRACTIONS

How exactly do we make space for creativity in such a distracted world? In a personal development seminar, author Brian Tracy said, "For success in life, turn things off." I believe that to not only listen to creativity, but actually hear it when it speaks, we must do the same. Below I've described the tools and apps that have supported my own efforts to minimize distractions.

### 1. Turn Off Your Phone or Leave It Out of the Room

This is one of the simplest creativity hacks, and I've used it on almost a daily basis. By turning off your phone, you shut off the inflow of noise, information, notifications, text messages, calls, and other sources of distraction. Schedule your "unplugged"

time each day and watch your ability to be more prolific, productive, and creative increase.

## 2. Eliminate the Need for Willpower

Too often we depend on willpower. But the problem with willpower is that it is limited. Simple daily decisions like what to
wear and what to eat reduce our willpower, resulting in what is
known as decision fatigue. As fatigue sets in, the decision to
avoid distractions becomes harder and harder. Fortunately tools
that help us to eliminate the need for willpower are available.

Focus is a simple free app that allows you to block distracting
websites and apps for a predetermined period of time.

RescueTime is a bit more sophisticated than Focus. While it
offers the same functionality, it also provides extensive reporting with statistics, such as how much time you spent on certain
websites or apps over the course of a day, a week, and even a
month. It provides a metric called your "productivity pulse,"
which measures the time you've spent each day on meaningful,
productive, and high-value activities. RescueTime allows you to
assign a productivity level to any website you visit or any app or
tool you use. Productivity levels range from "very distracting" to
"very productive."

In my own creative process, activities categorized as very
productive include:

- Using my distraction-free writing software (i.e., time spent
  working on my book or writing articles)

- Editing episodes of my podcast in GarageBand

- Using Keynote to design slides for talks that I'm giving

  Activities categorized as very distracting include:

- Visiting news websites, logging in to Facebook, Twitter, Instagram, or any other social network, and checking email

So rather than attempting to increase your followers on a social network, for example, try to improve your productivity pulse.

### 3. Use News Feed Eradicator

The Facebook News Feed Eradicator is a plug-in that eliminates the news feed, one of the biggest sources of distraction that keep people from getting anything done. But there are situations in which your use of Facebook might actually be required as part of your job. You might be a social media manager or, like me, use social media to share and promote your content. By using a tool like the News Feed Eradicator, you don't get sucked into clicking on things that people have posted and lose sight of why you actually logged on in the first place.

### 4. Work Analog Instead of Digital

I start most of my writing in a Moleskine notebook. I read physical books. Working analog forces you to slow down, and even causes you to retain more of what you've consumed.

In his book *Smarter Faster Better*, Charles Duhigg cited a study in which researchers gave students the same lecture and asked half of them to take notes by laptop and half to take notes by hand.

The students who took notes by laptop collected three times as much data because you can type much faster than you write. They would often type what the professor was saying verbatim.

Two weeks later, all the students took a test on the lecture material. Students who took notes by hand scored much higher than those who took notes on a laptop.

According to Duhigg, "the reason why is that the students who took notes by hand have had to work harder to collect that information. Oftentimes when you take notes by hand, you can't write as fast as the professor is speaking, you have to process what the professor is saying, and then put it in your own words on the piece of paper that you're writing on. As a result, you're transforming that information ... and that makes it much easier to remember and much easier to learn from."

When we choose to work analog instead of digital, we reduce our screen time. We increase the likelihood of in-person interaction and increase our ability to effectively read social cues. This is one of the many reasons why I recommend that you shouldn't turn your devices on first thing in the morning. You want to start your day and your creative work in a state of focus and flow, not in a scatterbrained state of anxiety fueled by distraction.

When we're not perpetually inundated with the dopamine-fueled hits that occur when we're connected, we become much more present and able to focus on the task at hand. And in turns we'll experience a reduction in our anxiety. By quite literally tuning out the noise, we reduce the likelihood of comparing ourselves to others, and minimize the anticipation of what might happen next in our inbox, on our Facebook profile, or on the social network of our choice.

But you don't have to take my word for the anxiety-reducing benefits of analog over digital.

Dr. Yalda Uhls, a child psychology researcher, conducted a five-day study of the effect on preteens of time away from screens. As explained on the website Anxiety.org:

> The goal of the experiment was to see if increasing opportunities of face-to-face interaction while eliminating face-to-screen interactions could improve nonverbal emotion-cue recognition in preteens. Uhls recruited 51 sixth graders from one public school in Southern California to participate in the experiment and 54 sixth graders from the same school were used as a control. During the pre-testing, Uhls found that both groups averaged spending four and a half hours each day texting, watching TV, and playing video games. Uhls and her team found that "children who were away from screens for five days with many opportunities for in-person interaction improved significantly in reading facial emotion."

With an understanding of how dopamine, distractions, and habit-forming products work to influence our behavior, we're equipped to create even more.

Technology can be either a source of distraction or a tool for creation. When we use it as a tool for creation rather than a vehicle for ego boosting, we end up living much more productive, prolific, and fulfilling creative lives.

## BE PROACTIVE WITH YOUR ENVIRONMENT

If you watch the evening or morning news, consider this: Most of the news is negative. The focus is almost entirely on crime, wars, and huge global problems. "Quite simply, good news doesn't catch our attention. Bad news sells because the amygdala is always looking for something to fear," says Peter Diamandis in *Abundance: The Future Is Better Than You Think*. So if bad news is part of your memetic environment, it will have a deleterious effect on your creative life.

Here are a few simple ways to improve your memetic environment.

**Unsubscribe** from everything in your inbox that isn't adding a significant amount of value to your life. Use a service like Unroll .Me to do this quickly. Do the same with podcasts, apps, and blogs you read. Because no equivalent Unroll.Me service exists for podcasts, I recommend that you unsubscribe from everything. Then choose what you want to put back. You'll discover that you were subscribed to many podcasts you weren't even listening to.

**Cut toxic ties.** People in your life either add or drain energy. Sadly, sometimes the people who drain our energy are close to us—

friends, family members, and significant others. In those cases we have to make incredibly difficult choices if we want to truly thrive. If they're not adding value to your life, if you don't like them, if you want nothing to do with them, it makes absolutely no sense to keep them. A friend of mine calls this "letting them rent space in your head." Your digital ties are one of the easiest places to begin upgrading your environment. While cutting these ties might feel painful initially, eventually you'll be really glad you did.

One of the dangers of having toxic ties is that they can stifle our creativity by causing us to water down our work or not say what we truly feel compelled to say out of fear of how they'll react. My friend and Unmistakable Creative guest Michael Gebben is someone I describe as the "Soup Nazi of Nice Guys." He has a zero tolerance policy for any negativity in his digital world. While it might sound harsh, I don't think I've ever seen a picture or a video of him without a smile on his face. And it's almost impossible not to like the guy.

**Choose a handful** of podcasts, newsletters, and blogs to read that add a tremendous amount of value to your life. I've found the following criteria useful for evaluating whether or not something adds value to my life:

- Does it inspire, educate, or entertain me?

- Does it move me toward the future or keep me stuck in the past?

- When I consume it, do I find myself feeling happier, more confident, and more secure? Or does it fuel my tendencies for comparison?

While it might seem strange, sometimes reading about other people's success actually hurts us more than it helps us. By paying attention to how something we consume makes us feel, we're able to differentiate between what helps us and what makes us feel worse.

For example, there are some successful bloggers who post income reports online. I noticed that every time I read one of their income reports, I would go into a mode of comparison and start feeling worse about my progress. I stopped reading their income reports—and my income went up.

I love Peter Diamandis's *Abundance Insider* newsletter because I learn about technologies of the future and about the mind-sets required for exponential growth. My Audible app is filled with inspiring biographies of visionary thinkers and entrepreneurs. (See Resources for my list.)

Treat the information you consume like the food you put into your body. If you are on a perpetual junk food binge, you're not going to feel very good. The same goes for your digital consumption habits.

## YOU IN YOUR ENVIRONMENT

What you actually do while you're in your environment also contributes to your creativity, for better or worse. Rituals, habits, and how you deploy your energy can strengthen your creative practice. Here's how to be proactive.

## RITUALS

The creative life is inherently uncertain. We can't predict the quality of our output or even what our ability to produce will be like on any given day. If you practice your creativity every day, you're inevitably going to have a few off times. Rituals give us something to count on and provide what author Jonathan Fields calls a "certainty anchor." Rituals allow us to be deliberate and to control at least one small aspect of our day, even if the rest of it feels like chaos. Rituals are a foundational element of a creative practice.

Our rituals also create an unconscious link to our environments. If you sit down at the same table at the same time every day and go through your ritual, whether that is reading a book with a cup of coffee, sculpting, or painting, eventually the environment and the ritual will be linked. For example, my brain knows that when I sit down at my table at six a.m., put on my headphones, and have my cup of coffee, it's time to write.

### DECISION FATIGUE

If you've ever been to the grocery store when you're hungry and tired, and you've packed your shopping cart full of weird food that you don't even eat, you've experienced one of the many unpleasant consequences of decision fatigue. Decision fatigue is the by-product of making too many decisions throughout the course of the day.

"The link between willpower and decision making works both ways: Decision-making depletes your willpower, and once your willpower is depleted, you're less able to make fewer decisions," says Roy Baumeister, coauthor with John Tierney of the book *Willpower*. The result is decision fatigue, and we're all prone to it. The average human being makes more than three hundred decisions each day: what to eat, what to wear, what websites to visit, what ads to click on. If you're involved in a complicated project, the number of decisions increases exponentially.

Rituals help us to reduce decision fatigue. When you don't have to decide what to wear, what to eat for breakfast, or something as simple as what pen you write with, you're able to preserve your willpower for what matters: your creative work.

To discover rituals that help you to eliminate decision fatigue, make a list of all your decisions in the first hour of your day. Then figure out how to ritualize each decision.

○ Consider planning what you're going to wear at the beginning of the week. Maybe you'll choose a certain color for each day of the week, or a certain style. The alternative is to follow in the footsteps of people like former president Barack Obama and Apple founder Steve Jobs and wear a version of a "uniform." If you decide to wear the same outfit every day, buy multiple versions of that outfit. (Otherwise you'll smell really bad or spend a lot of time doing laundry.)

○ For breakfast, eat the same thing every day or plan your meals in advance.

○ To start working, try using the same pen, the same paint-brush, or the same app or tool.

A ritual that effectively helps you to eliminate decision fatigue should be scripted enough that it will make the first hour of your day feel a bit like the movie *Groundhog Day* (without all the stress, anxiety, and meltdowns of Bill Murray).

Rituals also preserve our cognitive capabilities to achieve the kind of intensity of focus that is a precursor to flow. When we're not having to consciously focus on minutiae, we can shift all of that attention to here and now and to the task or creative habit at hand.

## RITUAL SPACE

A friend of mine has a ritual of going to the nicest hotels in town and writing in the lobby. The luxurious environment makes him feel abundant and energized. The way it makes you feel is one of the most important aspects of choosing your space. Other creatives have used this tactic as well. For example, I know of a visual artist who spent a summer sneaking into an old abandoned boat anchored in a harbor on eastern Long Island. At dusk, she'd sketch in the quiet, serene outdoor space that fed her soul.

Determine a space where your creative work will take place. It could be your kitchen table, an office in your home, or one of your favorite venues in your hometown. Be creative when it comes to settling on just the right spot for your creative practice.

## TIMING

Maybe you're a morning person who needs silence and solitude. Or you need the buzz of a coffee shop and the smell of freshly brewed coffee. Perhaps you're a night owl who does your best work when there's very little likelihood of interruption from the outside world. By knowing when we're at our best creatively, we can choose an ideal time for our creative ritual.

I do my best work between the hours of six and nine a.m. I brew my coffee, meditate, read for thirty minutes, and then open my Moleskine to a blank page and start writing whatever comes to mind. After filling up three to four pages, I'll usually open my laptop, transfer what I've written in my notebook, and keep writing until I get to a thousand words.

LISTEN TO: **STUART WILDE**

**Messy surroundings and an untidy life reflect a weakened metaphysical and psychological state. If you are powerful, you will dominate your life, you will find time to clean up and order things, and you will want to do that as a part of your personal discipline. Mess is the external manifestation of the ego's disquiet and laziness.**

Author Steven Pressfield has a different approach. He rises early, but rather than plunging into creative work, he begins the day with physical activity. "The theory is that it's not so much physical as it is psychological. I'm preparing myself for the day, for facing the resistance that I know I'm going to meet when I get into work," he wrote in a blog post.

Composer George Gershwin started the day with "a breakfast of eggs, toast, coffee, and orange juice, then immediately began composing sitting in his pajamas, bathrobe, and slippers," says Mason Currey, author of *Daily Rituals: How Artists Work*. He also made a habit of composing every day because if he "waited for the muse he would compose at most three songs a year."

Rituals, by definition, are very personal. You can't really adopt anyone else's rituals. Rather, you need to discover what works best for you. Often, creatives realize they have a ritual only in retrospect. I know a novelist who had to wear a certain yellow cashmere sweater whenever she wrote. After two years, she finished her novel and the sweater was literally in tatters. Whether it's lighting a scented candle before you sit down, saying a prayer of some sort, or drinking coffee from your favorite cup, make it yours and make it mindful.

## HABITS

Habits are the foundational building blocks of all creative work. Whether you're attempting to write a book, learn an instrument, build an iPhone app, or speak a new language, you will have to develop the habits that allow you to achieve your goal. In order for a habit to stick, it has to go from being an item on our to-do list to something we do without even having to consciously think about it. It has to become part of our identity.

The common pitfall that most people become victims of when adopting new habits is attempting to make drastic, unsustainable changes. As a result the habit doesn't stick. The easiest way to make a habit stick is by taking what our content strategist Kingshuk Mukherjee calls a "minimum viable action," which is the smallest possible thing you can do to reach your goal.

When people tell me that they want to write a thousand words a day but have never consistently done it, I encourage them to do nothing other than make a commitment to open their notebook each day. If they open their notebook for enough days in a row, they'll eventually realize they might as well write something. After they've consistently been able to open the notebook, I recommend they commit to a sentence, then a paragraph, then a page, and so on. Before long the simple act of opening their notebook has turned into a daily writing habit.

In an episode of *The Unmistakable Creative*, author and blogger James Clear told a story about a reader of his who wanted to develop the habit of exercising regularly. James encouraged him to just commit to driving to the gym. When he got to the gym, he decided to walk in. When he walked in, he figured he might as well work out. But the only thing he had committed himself to was driving to the gym. As a result he was able to follow through.

Your daily habits are part of the environment of *you*.

# ACTIVATION ENERGY

Activation energy is one of the most pivotal concepts you can learn to develop consistent creative habits. Based on the work of happiness researcher Shawn Achor, activation energy is a principle from physics that describes the effort required to take a particular action, a concept that we can apply to our creative habits. For an action we want to avoid, we have to increase the activation energy. For an action we want to take, we decrease the activation energy. By reducing the activation energy, we increase the likelihood that we'll follow through on whatever we've set out to do. By increasing the activation energy, we decrease the likelihood of doing something that we want to avoid.

## INCREASING ACTIVATION ENERGY TO AVOID DISTRACTION

Activation energy can help us to avoid distractions. When we use tools like RescueTime and Focus, we're increasing the activation energy by making it harder to access distracting websites and apps.

We can increase activation energy to avoid distracting apps on our smartphones in several ways:

1. **Delete the apps:** If you have to go through the effort of downloading a distracting app, due to an increase in activation energy, you'll be less inclined to use that app.

2. **Turn off all notifications and put the phone in Do Not Disturb mode:** By default, many of the apps that we use on a daily basis have notifications turned on. It's one of the many features that make the apps we use daily incredibly habit forming. By turning off notifications, we reduce the need for willpower and we're not perpetually interrupted every time somebody likes or comments on something. And if, like me, you use the phone for music while you're working, put the phone in Do Not Disturb mode and you won't be interrupted.

3. **Move apps off your home screen:** If you can't get yourself to delete the apps, and want to avoid mindless check-ins, consider moving distracting apps off your home screen. By nesting apps three or four screens deep you'll increase the activation energy and be less likely to use them.

4. **Switch your phone screen to gray scale:** It turns out that the most primitive part of the brain is highly responsive to colors, which is one of the reasons our phones are so irresistible. By changing our screens to gray scale, we reduce the temptation to check our phones so often.

5. **Use Flipd:** This is an iPhone app that disables distracting apps for a preset period of time. Once you turn it on, you won't

have access to any distracting apps on your phone until the time block you've set is over.

You can take the same approach on your computer. By removing shortcuts to distracting applications from our desktops and web browsers, you reduce the likelihood of giving in to distractions.

If distraction is the enemy of creativity, focus and flow are its essential nutrients.

## REDUCING ACTIVATION ENERGY TO FUEL CREATIVITY

We can fuel creativity and see significant increases in our productivity when we reduce activation energy.

Understanding activation energy played a pivotal role in how I developed a daily writing habit. By setting my notebook out on my desk the night before, I reduce activation energy because I don't have to get it off the shelf. I open up my writing software on my computer the night before, so it's the first thing I see when I turn on my laptop. By not having to click on the application to open it, I've reduced the activation energy—it may sound like very little but it's a cumulative saving of seconds that makes a difference, at least psychologically.

- If you want to practice a musical instrument, put it somewhere you'll see it and you'll be much more likely to practice it.

- If you want to paint daily, put your brushes and canvases in your line of sight.

- If you want to become a prolific photographer, put the icon for your camera app on the home screen of your smartphone.

By eliminating just a few simple steps, you significantly increase the likelihood that you'll follow through on a desired creative habit.

## DELIBERATE PRACTICE

Mastery of any craft requires deliberate practice. It can become easy to go through the motions of a creative habit and delude yourself into thinking that you're engaging in deliberate practice. Deliberate practice is not simply repeating a task until you've reached the ten-thousand-hour mark Malcolm Gladwell made famous.

"At the driving range or at the piano, most of us, as adults, are just doing what we've done before and hoping to maintain the level of performance that we reached long ago," says author Geoff Colvin. "By contrast deliberate practice requires that one identify certain sharply defined elements of performance that need to be improved and work intently on them."

Professor Anders Ericsson first coined the term "deliberate practice." Ericsson and his colleagues studied violin students at the Berlin Music Academy in order to discover "what sorts of achievement might be possible with rigorous formal training methods" and to "understand what separated the truly outstanding violinists from those who were merely good." Their study, "The Role of Deliberate Practice in the Acquisition of Expert Performance," revealed that even among the most gifted of musicians, those who had committed more time to deliberate practice were far more accomplished. In his book *Peak: Secrets from the New Science of Expertise,* Ericsson proposes the following guidelines for deliberate practice:

- Deliberate practice develops skills that other people have already figured out how to do and for which effective training techniques have been established.

- Deliberate practice involves well-defined specific goals and often involves improving some aspect of the target performance.

- Deliberate practice is deliberate—that is, it requires a person's full attention and conscious actions.

- Deliberate practice involves feedback and modification efforts in response to that feedback.

- Deliberate practice both produces and depends on effective mental representations.

*At All Costs* is a documentary film about youth basketball players at the most elite levels. Part of the documentary focuses on the journey of a then–high school point guard named Parker Jackson-Cartwright. His training regimen is a perfect example of deliberate practice.

He works one-on-one with a coach on specific aspects of his

game that need improvement, attends basketball camps hosted by NBA players, and plays in the AAU basketball league during the summer outside of his regular season. In the middle of the film he suffers an injury that takes him off the court for four months. By the end of the film, he receives an NCAA Division I basketball scholarship.

Given that this book is about the value of creativity for its own sake, you may wonder why I've emphasized the importance of mastery and deliberate practice. So often we have ideas of what we want to create: books we'd love to write, projects we'd like to initiate, or companies we dream of starting. But at our current skill level, we're not capable of executing our vision. The ability to create what we want to see exist in the world and have it meet our highest standards requires both deliberate practice and mastery. "Skill gives you wherewithal to execute what occurs to you. Without it you are just a font of unfulfilled ideas," writes choreographer Twyla Tharp.

I learned Tharp's lesson as a high school freshman from my ninth-grade band director. I had been rehearsing the tuba endlessly for the all-region orchestra and band auditions. I was staying after school for three hours, and because we lived in a small apartment at the time, I would practice in our minivan in the mornings. Much to the dismay of my family and my sister (due to the loud sustained booming sounds), I was extremely committed to getting good at the tuba.

In November, I auditioned for the all-region orchestra and it was a disaster. Despite all my practice, the performance was subpar. After that audition my band director had me do something that seemed incredibly counterintuitive. Rather than play the piece exactly as it sounded on the tape that had been recorded by a professional tuba player, he had me slow it down drastically. Instead of tempo, we focused on accuracy. If there was a measure that I wasn't playing correctly, we would commit an entire afternoon to that measure until I got it right.

We would take the mouthpiece off the instrument and play sections solely with the mouthpiece. This actually came in handy when our family had to take a weeklong trip to California prior to my dad's appointment as a professor at the University of California, Riverside. It was one week before the all-region auditions and we couldn't lug the tuba along. So for that whole week, I practiced using only my mouthpiece. By the time December had rolled around and I auditioned for the all-region band, I had gone from a subpar performance to being second chair in the all-region band and had advanced to auditions for the all-state band.

LISTEN TO: **KARL OVE KNAUSGAARD**

In a state of flow, the activity in the frontal lobe is reduced, it is almost shut down—and it is in the frontal lobe the ability for abstract thinking is situated, the planning for the future and the sense of self. Everything that makes us human, in other words, and that makes perfect sense: You lose yourself and sink into a state of pure being, like an animal— belonging to the world, not to yourself.

If you look at my band director's methods, you'll notice the elements of deliberate practice at work.

By focusing on individual measures and playing certain parts of the music with just my mouthpiece, I could identify clearly defined elements of my performance that needed improvement and could work intently on them. He was also attempting to modify my performance in response to his feedback. Through his musical knowledge, he was using effective training techniques that had already been established.

My ninth-grade band director deserves far more credit than he gets for the role that he's played in the consistency of my creative habit.

For me as a writer, deliberate practice has meant slowing down. The most frequent comment that my collaborator Robin Dellabough would make to me in the process of writing two books was "slow it down." Or to put it more bluntly, "verbal vomit" does not constitute deliberate practice. It took me a while to truly understand what she meant. Slowing down meant laboring over two words in a sentence, supporting everything I had said with more evidence, avoiding repetition, and in some cases, rewriting much of what I'd already written. Funnily enough, it's as if the advice of my band director had come full circle in my writing life.

The lesson for our creativity is simply this: To make our most ambitious creative dreams come true, deliberate practice has to be part of the picture.

## FLOW: THE GIFT AND GIVER OF CREATIVITY

At the heart of any athletic, professional, or creative endeavor or achievement is flow. It causes entrepreneurs to keep starting companies, artists to keep making art, and athletes to keep pushing their own limitations. Flow amplifies ambition, not because of the external reward or recognition, but because nothing produces the same level of joy as being so deeply absorbed in an endeavor. It is a state in which "we are aligned with our core passion, and because of flow's incredible impact on performance, expressing that passion to our utmost," says author Steven Kotler. As I mentioned in Part Two, flow is one of the main reasons that our creativity plays such a pivotal role in our happiness.

Flow is not precisely a habit, but you can manipulate your habits in such a way that you can allow for more flow. For example, certain activities are conducive to flow and others are not. Generally, flow starts to occur during deep work: something that is rare, valuable, meaningful, and cognitively demanding.

Reading a book, writing a book, computer programming, and practicing a musical instrument all fall into the category of deep work. Mindlessly browsing the internet, chatting with friends, and so many of the things that compete for our attention are considered shallow work. A simple filter is the following:

Is this activity going to add meaning and value to my life? Is it something that will make me better for having done it?

If the answer is no, it's probably shallow work and won't produce flow.

## FLOW TRIGGERS

Whereas the feeling of flow is magical, the ability to access the state is more mechanical than magical. It requires a combination of several factors that are known as "flow triggers."

The first prerequisites for flow are focus and attention. True focus means doing one thing at a time. If you place a magnifying glass over a piece of paper in the hot sun, it catches fire. When you narrow your focus with intensity to a singular task, you ignite the spark that leads to flow.

The chatter of your mind starts to decrease in volume because your mind is fully occupied. As a result you're able to listen to yourself more effectively, which in turn produces significant creative breakthroughs, insights, and a profound sense of fulfillment.

Given that flow follows focus, a singular focus in all of our daily activities makes it easier to experience flow when we do creative work. In the process, the ability to maintain singular focus becomes a habit. So in addition to creative activities, aim for singular focus in all your daily activities, even checking email, browsing the web, uploading pictures, or updating your status. When you multitask, you shorten your attention span and decrease your productivity. You also inhibit your ability to return to flow when you're done with these activities.

Try to "mono-task" to improve your focus and attention.

Make a to-do list of all the things that you'd like to get done to-day, including high-value creative work like writing, painting, or taking photos on your list. Also include updating your status on Facebook, responding to emails, and uploading pictures to Instagram. You'll find you're able to get everything on your list done faster when you're working on only one at a time.

I've noticed this pattern over and over in my own work. If I am editing an episode of my podcast, and I try to check email, check Facebook, check Twitter, and then edit the podcast, it takes up to ninety minutes. If I focus on nothing other than editing the podcast, I can have it edited, uploaded, and ready to publish in about thirty minutes.

Below are a few simple tools and hacks that enable you to more easily focus on a single task.

- OneTab is a browser extension for Google Chrome that prevents you from being able to open more than one browser tab at a time, so you can't have Facebook and email open at the same time.

- Full-screen mode: If something is in your line of sight, you're much more likely to have your attention shift to it. Full-screen mode is a way of increasing activation energy by taking things out of your line of sight. By working in full-screen mode, you're forced to use only one application at a time.

- Consider the setup of your physical space and what it is you're attempting to accomplish. For example, if you're reading a book, have nothing but that book on the desk. If you're painting, have nothing but the canvas and the paintbrush you need. Ask yourself what single resource you need access to in order to complete your task and limit yourself to only that.

## THE CHALLENGE/SKILLS RATIO

In order for what we're working on to feel effortless, it initially has to require effort and challenge us. It has to stretch us without breaking us, the midpoint between boredom and anxiety. "[Flow] often requires strenuous physical exertion or highly disciplined mental activity. It does not happen without skilled performance," says psychologist Mihaly Csikszentmihalyi.

This is why it takes a writer a thousand words, a basketball player a series of made shots, a surfer a few good waves, and a snowboarder a few good runs before flow kicks in. If it's too easy, we'll get bored and quit. If it's too hard, we'll be paralyzed and never get into flow.

The challenge/skills ratio also provides us with an incentive to master our craft without concern for a positive external outcome. The greater our skill level at whatever our art form is, the more likely that making our art will result in flow.

When we take a risk of any kind, there are potential downsides and significant upsides. Risk creates a heightened sense of awareness and presence. This ensures a challenge/skills ratio that is conducive to flow.

This is why we see action sports athletes chase bigger thrills, entrepreneurs attempt to solve more ambitious problems, and artists continually attempt to stretch their creative capacities. The greater the risk, the greater the reward; the result is more flow.

At a certain point the challenge/skills ratio changes due to the fact that our skill level has increased. Thus we have to adjust the flow triggers accordingly.

**FLOW OF TIME**

The relationship of time to flow is a paradox. Time appears to fly by when we're in a state of flow, but it actually takes time to reach the state. This initial window of time can feel boring, as if time is standing still, and is often when the craving for a shot of dopamine and the temptation to give in to a source of distraction is highest.

In my own creative practice, I've found that it can take anywhere between thirty and forty-five minutes to achieve flow. During that period, I have jokingly said that my words are "all coming out the wrong end." But shortly after that, I'm able to find the words for what I'm trying to say more easily, I'm able to construct sentences effortlessly, and I feel much more lucid. Author Sally Hogshead reaffirmed this idea in an episode of *The Unmistakable Creative* when she said, "I know my best writing doesn't happen in the first hour, but in the second and third hour."

When we reach the second and third hour, time dissolves,

and to stop working feels like walking away from a blackjack table when you're on a hot streak. In other words, don't stop working when you've managed to achieve flow.

## UNINTERRUPTED CREATION

Interruptions both inhibit reaching flow and take us out of flow. Anything that requires you to shift your attention from what you're working on to something else effectively requires you to start the entire thirty-to-forty-five-minute cycle all over again.

Comedian Dave Chappelle produced a skit with the premise "Imagine if the internet was a place in the physical world that you could actually go to." The skit showed him walking through what looked like a mall, with the stores and other people in the mall as the equivalent of websites and pop-up ads. Between pirated music, anatomical extension opportunities, and more, it exemplified information overload. By the end of the skit Chappelle had more or less lost his mind.

The modern world is much like the one Chappelle made fun of—a shouting match filled with people who are trying to get our attention and constantly interrupting us. We click on things with no idea why. One link leads us down a rabbit hole of a dozen more and we've spent an hour researching, say, "Spirit Cooking" while doing a Google search about elected officials. (True story.)

Interruptions force our inner voice to compete for our attention. In order to listen to ourselves, our creation time must be completely uninterrupted. That's why I never take phone calls or meetings between six and ten a.m. My agent, my editor, and even my team members never call me or attempt to meet with me during the early morning. I use the Focus@Will app with noise cancellation headphones so that I can't be interrupted by doorbells ringing, people in my house yelling, or another customer at Starbucks who wants to chat.

## CLEAR GOALS AND IMMEDIATE FEEDBACK

Clear goals play an important role in flow because they provide a target and narrow our focus. Consider the difference between the following two items on a to-do list:

1. Sit down and write.

2. Write one thousand words or write for one hour.

If you just "sit down and write" there's no way to know whether you've actually accomplished your goal. But one thousand words or one hour is very concrete. You hit your word count/time limit or you don't. You can measure or evaluate your time. Clear goals also provide a semblance of control: We focus on what we're trying to accomplish with intention and purpose.

Immediate feedback is built into certain activities. For example, a musician playing a piece of music immediately hears what he's playing and can determine where there might be room for improvement. Surfers in the ocean, snowboarders on mountains, and other action sports athletes get immediate feedback because they're immersed in nature, which is continuously changing.

For activities that don't necessarily have immediate built-in feedback, clear goals become even more important. If you're a writer, a daily word count or specific number of paragraphs allows you to combine a clear goal and receive immediate feedback, both in the form of progress toward it and when you hit that goal.

If you're a visual artist, develop an image in your head of what a completed piece of work looks like. As the work progresses, compare what you're seeing on the canvas with the image in your head.

As long as "it is logically related to a goal in which one has invested psychic energy," says Mihaly Csikszentmihalyi, it can serve as a form of immediate feedback and a flow trigger.

**MEASURE YOUR EFFORT**

How exactly do you measure your progress on a daily basis? To do so you need certain parameters:

1. Is it in your control?

2. Is it something that you can easily measure?

3. Is it actually attainable?

The reason that I use one thousand words a day as my main metric for writing is because it's a way to assess progress that I can control, easily measure, and attain.

Another method that creatives use to measure their growth was popularized by comedian Jerry Seinfeld. Seinfeld encouraged a younger comedian to put up a calendar and on the days that he wrote a joke to put an *X* on the calendar. Eventually there would be a chain, and the goal from that point forward was not to break the chain. Whereas this method might seem simple, I've found that it is also very effective. Having a visual reminder of your creative momentum can be incredibly powerful.

As part of his deep work philosophy, Cal Newport recommends that people keep a compelling scoreboard. One example of this kind of scoreboard is the "don't break the chain" method mentioned here. A scoreboard "provides a reinforcing source of motivation" and causes you to "become invested in perpetuating this performance."

## PASSION

When I look at the work of the most fulfilled creatives I know, one pattern keeps emerging: their happiness and their creativity are correlated. In my own life, I know it's true. If I plotted out my happiness levels on a graph, the peaks would all be times when I was making or building something that I cared deeply about. When we're not creative, there's an unmet need inside of us that starts to go dormant. And as that need goes dormant, the world doesn't appear as vibrant, our hearts don't race as much, and our eyes lose their luster.

To say that I hated my first job out of college, working in inside sales at a software company, would be an understatement. It negatively affected my health, and I was fired five days before Christmas.

At the same time I was struggling to stay in such a bad job, a friend from college started a website called *Summer of Amit*, basically a blog before they were called blogs. He invited several of our other classmates to be contributors on the site, including me. Thus a daily piece that affectionately became known as "Summer of Srini" was born. I wrote about our company's ridiculous antics, from the guy who tried to beat me up at the hometown buffet to the CEO who went on a rampage each month and fired people. I wrote about the toxic working environment in the hopes of making my friends laugh.

LISTEN TO: **RAINER MARIA RILKE**

This most of all: ask yourself in the most silent hour of your night: must I write? Dig into yourself for a deep answer. And if this answer rings out in assent, if you meet this solemn question with a strong, simple "I must," then build your life in accordance with this necessity; your whole life, even into its humblest and most indifferent hour, must become a sign and witness to this impulse. Then come close to Nature.

By the end of the summer, I was the most prolific contributor to the website. Even though I had no idea that I was planting some of the early seeds for my life as a writer, that daily opportunity to write and share it with my friends became a source of sanity. It made the experience of working a job that I dreaded going to a bit more tolerable. Every circumstance can give you colors or notes that you can apply creatively. It's all material.

After completing a project or phase or book, a sort of postpartum depression sets in, a certain nostalgia for being right in the middle, consumed by whatever I'm working on. There's immeasurable value to these moments, the creative equivalent of nirvana, of heaven and beauty combined that doesn't compare to the book on a shelf, the praise of fans, and other sources of external validation. And it turns out I'm not alone.

The most prolific creators, those who make meaningful work on a regular basis, are those who derive the most satisfaction and value from their work. Author Dani Shapiro has written multiple books, has had a thriving twenty-plus-year career, and has achieved what many authors might consider the pinnacle of creative success, an appearance on Oprah's *SuperSoul Sunday*. But there's been no moment of arrival, when the work is all done. In her fittingly titled book *Still Writing: The Perils and Pleasures of a Creative Life,* she says, "What I do know—what I've spent the past couple of decades learning about myself—is that if I'm not writing, I'm not well. If I'm not writing, the world around me is slowly leached of its color."

Creativity enables us not just to express, but to experience the wide range of human emotions that are part of what my friend author Pam Slim calls "a full-color, full-contact life." It's a life in which we let go of our expectations and operate from a place of imagination and curiosity, while being open to the possibilities of where our creativity will lead us. We might take waves on the head and punches to the face. We're just as likely to catch a perfect wave and deliver a knockout performance. A full-color, full-contact life is a soulful exploration of what we hold dear, in our hearts and in our minds.

The lesson is that even when the lights go out and the curtains close, the work itself is the ultimate source of our happiness. Writer Neil Gaiman says work is "the ultimate lifesaver" that "gets you through the good times, and gets you through the other ones." In other words, your passion is your motor.

Passion emerges from exploration and experimentation, and a willingness to embrace uncertainty. "You will never be successful unless you embrace the process of discovery and accept uncertainty," says Tina Seelig. Passion also emerges from sticking with something long enough that we become skilled at it.

If you had asked me eight years ago, when I started recording conversations with bloggers, if I was passionate about interviewing people, the answer would have been no. The more I did, however, the better I became at it, and the more I found it engaging. Because it was engaging, what emerged was a passion for storytelling through interviews. With a combination of engagement and passion, what followed was flow.

Passion follows engagement, meaning follows mastery, and flow follows both.

## SWITCHING UP YOUR ENVIRONMENT: RENEWAL AND RECOVERY

Part of listening to yourself is knowing when you need time to recover, and ideas need time to bake. In an always on, constantly connected world, the lines between work and play have all been blurred. Hustling and crushing it is considered a badge of honor. It's rare for anybody to proudly state that they did "nothing."

No matter how many hours you're able to put in and how much you're able to produce on a consistent basis, you have to build in periods of creative renewal or your work will inevitably suffer. Research shows that periods of rest and renewal can actually result in creative breakthroughs. "When we are in a frenzy, frantically searching for answers, we do more to handicap our minds than to actually solve the problem; we are pushing our brains to the limits and failing to discover fresh insights," and "connections are built when brain activation slows and even when our brain is at rest," says Sandra Bond Chapman, director of the Center for BrainHealth at the University of Texas at Dallas.

One of the challenges I faced in writing this book was that I didn't have the same momentum as I had on my previous book.

Despite my writing a thousand words every day, so little of it was usable that the process was much slower than my usual pace. In my frustration, I tried longer hours and higher word counts, largely to no avail. I resisted the temptation to throw my laptop against the wall (I'm convinced all writers face that urge at one time or another).

Right before beginning this section on rest, I spent a weekend away in Montana in an area with no cell service or internet access. When I got back to the airport to go home and sat down, I found it much easier to write than I had for the entire month before. After that I was convinced of the virtues of rest, recovery, and being completely unplugged from the world.

"Your ability to work at a high level is like fitness. If you never took a break between sets, you wouldn't be able to build strength, stamina, and endurance. However, not all 'rest' produces recovery. Certain things are more soothing than others," says writer Benjamin Hardy. For example, if we decide to go for an afternoon walk, but spend the entirety of the walk texting people and uploading photos to Instagram, any benefits we might experience from such a renewal effectively get cancelled out.

Within your daily practice, listen for an inevitable point of diminishing returns, a point during the day when your efforts decline in both quality and quantity. When you hit this point of diminishing returns, your focus, productivity, and creativity all plummet.

When I started my habit of writing a thousand words a day,

after a few weeks I noticed a pattern of my best work being done early in the morning, and a steady decline in my capabilities after about twelve p.m. Thus my mornings are utilized for my most important creative work and my afternoons are set aside for rest, renewal, and recovery.

The way to determine your own point of diminishing returns is to immerse yourself in a creative habit of some sort for enough days in a row that you've collected data points. Think of yourself as a social scientist who is studying your own behavior. With enough data points, you'll be able to uncover patterns and determine what your optimal times are for renewal, recovery, and rest.

When I was writing my previous book, I would completely shut down in the middle of the afternoon on a daily basis, go to Starbucks, and then take a walk while reviewing the latest episode of *The Unmistakable Creative*, which often served as inspiration for many of the ideas in the book. Then I would come back and jot things down in a notebook, on note cards, and in Evernote.

Any time you feel depleted, uninspired, or even on the cusp of burnout, consider doing at least one of the following:

**Travel**—to the next town, state, or country—it really doesn't matter as long as you're changing your scenery. When we experience the same scenery day after day, we sometimes get caught up in repetitive thought patterns. "We have to keep changing the channels in our brains because if we don't do that we'll get stuck in rhythms that we don't necessarily want," says Unmistakable Creative Dave Vanderveen.

**Take a "staycation"** with activities you don't normally do. Consider checking into a hotel in your own town for a few days. Book a massage, have a nice dinner, and treat yourself like royalty for a day or two. While I was working on the final revisions for my previous book, a friend of mine had an apartment in Santa Barbara that he was not spending very much time at because his fiancé lived in San Francisco. He sent me the keys in the mail and I spent an entire weekend at his house putting the final touches on the manuscript.

**Explore your own neighborhood** by walking or taking public transportation. Go to a different coffee shop or restaurant other than your regular spot. "If you keep going where you always go, you will have a progressively less interesting experience over time. We get desensitized and the novelty wears off," says Jon Levy in his book *The 2 AM Principle: Discover the Science of Adventure.* When you make a deliberate choice to explore your neighborhood, you'll be amazed by what's been right in front of your eyes but which you've somehow never noticed.

Nothing has a more profound impact on us than the environments we inhabit. From the spaces we live in to the information we consume and the people we surround ourselves with, our environment is the world in which we're immersed. The quality of our environments will ultimately determine what we're able to express. The environment in which you create is sacred. Stand guard at the door of it. Don't let in toxic people or information, unpleasant sounds or sights, uncomfortable objects or clothing. Your work and your life will become the fullest expression of your environment. Treat it accordingly.

# UNMISTAKABLE PRACTICE:
## ACTIVITIES AND EXERCISES

### LISTEN TO THE RIGHT MUSIC

For the next week or two, experiment with different genres of music. Play at least three songs or sections of each genre, listening carefully to your reactions. Does one song sound melancholy or upbeat? Meditative or energetic? Disturbing or restful? Be careful to try genres outside your usual taste. If you always play jazz, try country. If you always listen to classical, try Broadway show tunes. Or, within a genre, expand your horizons. Maybe you've played Katy Perry, Lady Gaga, and the Backstreet Boys until you've practically memorized them. So today, try Bob Dylan, Dave Matthews, and U2.

### THE SEVEN TIMES THREE MEDITATION

This simple meditation technique works on several levels. First, like any meditation, it focuses and quiets your mind, which will help prime your creative pump and prepare you to enter a state of flow. It also makes you more deeply aware of your environment in a very specific way.

Start by sitting comfortably wherever you usually do your creative work. Close your eyes and take a few easy breaths.

Now gently open your eyes and count seven things you can see around you: light in a window, a chair, your dog.

Next, count seven things you can hear: the refrigerator whirring, a siren, birds.

Finally, count seven things you can feel: wind, the fabric of a pillow, your skin.

Now count six things you can see. They can include items from the first counting, but you may also see something you hadn't noticed before.

Count six sounds.

Count six things you can feel.

Keep doing this, each time with one less item. Count five things you can see, five things you can hear, five things you can feel, then four, three, two, and finally one.

Go slowly and notice your final sight, sound, and feeling. Are they pleasant? Interesting? Soothing? Disturbing? If you don't like a sight or sound, can you change it somehow? Get rid of the ugly poster you never liked or hang heavier curtains to muffle the traffic noise? You create in an environment, so make it as custom fit to your individual needs and tastes as possible.

## PLAYDATES

*The Artist's Way* includes taking time once a week to go on what Julia Cameron calls "artist's dates." I love her idea and suggest that you make it part of your creative habit, too. It's a simple concept: You schedule a specific time to take yourself on a little field trip of pure delight and pleasure. The only "rule" is that the date can't feel like work. Other than that, you're free to explore and discover however and wherever your spirit takes you. Maybe swinging at a child's playground is your idea of bliss. Or browsing in a bead and ribbon store. Maybe it's more obvious—a museum exhibit or a documentary about an artist you admire. Sometimes you set out to see a specific show and stumble on the unexpected, like my friend Zoey. A poet, she was feeling a need to replenish her store of words and images. She found an Alfred Sisley exhibit nearby. The bonus was an adjacent part of the small museum, filled with examples of crystals from around the world. The next morning, as she started writing, she had a virtual word quarry to mine.

Whatever you choose, your playdates will be a reward, a positive reinforcement that you're feeding your creative self. That's why Cameron says to make your dates solo and regular.

## MAKE SOMETHING EVERY DAY

You may have heard of a 365 photography project or a thirty-day writing challenge. The idea is that you make a commitment to creating within a genre on a daily basis. You can find dozens of these self-directed competitions online, but it might be even more fun and creative to customize your own. Maybe it's as simple as making a recipe every day until you've gone through one entire cookbook, the way Julie Powell gave herself one year to cook her way through *Mastering the Art of French Cooking*. Noah Scalin created a skull in different media and forms every day for a year. Other possibilities include:

- Making origami daily for ninety days

- Building a cairn (a balanced tower of stones) once a week for a year

- Writing a postcard to someone every day

- Knitting seventeen hats in 2017 or eighteen scarves in 2018

- Making and recording some kind of music every day

## SOCIAL FASTING

I'd like to encourage you to try the following simple two-part experiment.

Step One:
*Quit social media for one entire day. Use a tool like RescueTime to block all distracting websites.*

Step Two:
*The next day, spend as much time as you possibly can on Facebook, Twitter, or Instagram. Check your email every time you're tempted to. While you're at it, make sure you have all your notifications on your phone turned on.*

Compare the difference in your levels of anxiety, productivity, and creative output between both days. This will give you a very visceral experience of what it feels like when your brain is on the internet. What you'll likely discover is that the first day produces less anxiety and is far more fulfilling.

## CREATIVE CROSS-TRAINING

In athletics, cross-training is working on some element of performance that will improve your primary sport. For example, if a surfer lifts weights, he builds upper body strength to be able to paddle and push himself up on waves. The point of creative cross-training is to immerse yourself for a short period of time in a pursuit outside your usual activities. Through experimentation and immersion, we open ourselves up to creative breakthroughs and insights that might never have otherwise occurred. We build unused creative muscles.

If you're a painter, take a cooking class.

If you're a poet, try sketching instead.

Other creative cross-training ideas might include:

- Learning how to weld

- Taking an improv class

- Teaching yourself computer coding

- Making up a new dance

My own creative cross-training efforts have included thirty days of teaching myself how to draw, doing street photography, and spray painting planets, galaxies, and silhouettes of surfers.

# PART FOUR

# LISTENING TO OTHERS

n early 2017, my business partner, Brian, and I set a goal to attend a Singularity University program. Its mission is to help people build companies and nonprofit initiatives. However, given the substantial price for the two-week executive course, we had to shelve the idea. A few weeks later, founder Peter Diamandis opened up a digital version of the same curriculum. For about $800 we gleaned the wisdom and insights of someone who has built several successful companies; is at the leading edge of new technologies like artificial intelligence, 3-D printing, and human longevity; and is on a mission to help people build companies that will affect a billion people within a decade.

Today we have virtually unrestricted access to some of the brightest minds in the world. We can listen to and learn from creative professionals, coaches, entrepreneurs, and venture capitalists. It would be foolish not to take advantage of what is effectively a collective consciousness.

Anything of significance is achieved with the help of others. To push beyond the limits of what we currently believe is possible with our creative efforts, we have to learn to listen to each teacher we encounter. In any great creator's work you'll find the traces of people who have inspired them, giants whose shoulders they've stood on, and teachers who have passed on their wisdom. In those we admire we see a reflection, not of our current selves, but of who we aspire to become.

In listening to others we prime our creative pump. Our creative work is informed by the books we read, the art we see, and the company we keep. What we put into that creative stew is entirely up to us. As author Dani Shapiro said in *Still Writing*, "Every good book you'll ever read has the thumbprints of other writers all over it."

Without the insight and input of others, we develop tunnel vision and become close-minded. A limited mind eventually results in limited possibilities. To listen to others requires us to set aside our egos, put our hubris on the shelf, and adopt an attitude of humility. To become a master of any craft, you must become a perpetual student and lifelong learner.

While listening to others is essential to the creative process, it does have a dark side. When we start to listen to others so much that we're running our lives and our work by consensus and committee, we run the risk of doing great harm to our work. We give away our power, and in that process lose the unmistakable signature that we're capable of bringing to anything we create. Not only that, we're stuck with the results of somebody else's choices. It's not uncommon for people to attempt a new marketing tactic or trick that was recommended by a peer, denying their own instincts, only to regret the action and the results that follow.

In her book *White Hot Truth,* Danielle LaPorte says, "If you really want to mess up your life, never question spiritual authorities." And I'd say if you really want to kill your creative life, never question authority in general. When we don't have the courage to question authority, direction turns into dogma. Part of listening to others is knowing when to question what they're telling us.

Elizabeth DiAlto, creator of the Wild Soul Movement, launched a membership site for her community. By all accounts it was a success. Members of her community loved it and it was profitable. But she didn't enjoy it. She described it as "a digital version of having to show up to a job at the same time all the time." In our conversation she said, "Every now and then I get seduced by things other people do that I'm not built for." Eventually she shut down the site and issued refunds.

When listening to others makes our creative work feel less like a privilege and more like an obligation, it might be time to reconsider their opinions and listen to ourselves. For those of us who have a natural tendency to please others, knowing when not to listen to others can be difficult. But when we are out of alignment with our soul's calling, it's the artistic equivalent of voluntarily putting ourselves in what surfers refer to as the impact zone. Rather than catching waves, we're gluttons for punishment who choose to take them head-on.

There are times, however, when it makes sense to listen to others, a time when we need their support, inspiration, energy, and cheerleading. When you're stuck they can help you get unstuck. When you're unclear they can help you find clarity. Listening to others begins with connection and community.

## CONNECTION, SUPPORT, AND COMMUNITY

Many creators, including me, have a tendency to go into a cave when working on a big project. Everything other than the work is a distraction. We're more connected than we've ever been and yet we're lonelier than we've ever been. But to sustain creativity, we need support and community.

- Teams free us up to focus on our strongest skill set.

- A creative partner can enable us to accomplish far more than we could on our own.

- Virtual and in-person communities give us opportunities to meet like-minded people, learn from people who have walked the path before us, and enjoy benefits from their support.

By building teams, finding creative partners, and turning to online and in-person communities, we ensure that we don't become completely isolated during the creative process. Listening to others is equally as significant as any other form of listening.

## CREATIVE PARTNERS: TWO-PERSON TEAMS

One of the great myths of creativity is that of the lone creator or genius. In studying creative teams, author Geoff Colvin discovered that "each consists of a boss who became famous and a much less famous number 2 who devoted his career to the success of the enterprise." You see the result of creative collaboration in dozens of creative two-person teams.

A creative duo from the entertainment world is Matt Damon and Ben Affleck, who collaborated on the Oscar-winning film *Good Will Hunting*. The partnership began in high school when they began holding meetings during lunch and established a joint bank account to fund their trips to New York City for auditions. When they watched a movie with their friends, even if it was terrible, Affleck would share what he thought would have made it better.

In addition to writing together, they both sang each other's praises to the movie directors they auditioned for. Reflecting on the success of *Good Will Hunting* and his partnership with Affleck, in a conversation with *Off Camera* host Sam Jones, Damon said, "When the movie came out, because my part was bigger and I played a genius, people thought that I must have done more of the work," but "we could not have done it without each other."

In Damon and Affleck, we see a number of traits that make it possible for creative pairs to succeed: a strong friendship that had been built over many years, a lack of envy of each other's success, and a willingness to speak on each other's behalf when it came to opportunities for leading roles. Their generosity of spirit strengthened their creative spirit.

LISTEN TO: **MICHAEL JORDAN**

**My greatest skill was being teachable. I was like a sponge. Even if I thought my coaches were wrong, I tried to listen and learn something.**

Danielle Weisberg and Carly Zakin, cofounders of the daily newsletter *The Skimm*, are another powerful creative team. They met while studying abroad in Rome; several years later, they reconnected and became "professional storytellers, as producers for NBC News—working in breaking news, political news, and documentaries." Eventually they became friends and roommates as well as colleagues. Their mutual passion for news and stories led to the formation of *The Skimm*, which today reaches millions and whose readers include celebrities like Oprah Winfrey.

The right partners expand your creative universe. What once appeared impossible suddenly becomes doable. What makes for great creative pairs? How do they stay productive instead of becoming competitive? And what leads to the dissolution of certain partnerships?

## CONFIDENCE, TRUST, AND COMMITMENT

Confidence and trust are two of the most critical elements to the success of any creative pair. You have to have confidence that the other person is not only capable of doing what they say they will, but will actually do it. This is also how trust is built. "For pairs to jell, it's essential that confidence deepen over time, that each find the other reliable," says Joshua Wolf Shenk, author of *Powers of Two*. You want your creative partner to have a pattern of following through and an equal level of commitment to the success of the partnership. When one person is doing all the work in a partnership and the other is simply along for the ride, the partnership inevitably will disintegrate.

## THE DREAMER AND THE DOER

In many creative pairs the dreamer is the one with an endless array of ideas, while the doer makes the execution of those ideas possible. It's not that the dreamer doesn't do any work. In fact, a dreamer does just as much work. But doers keep dreamers focused. And each has some tendencies of the other, which amplifies creativity in both of them.

## NO EGO OR ENVY

For a creative pair to succeed, nobody in the pair can put themselves above the other. Ego and envy must be out of the equation. If one person is envious of the success of the other, that envy can quickly turn into resentment, while ego and a sense of entitlement can destroy a fruitful partnership. Creative pairs have to celebrate each other's success and achievements in order to thrive. "We're in this together" is the attitude that successful creative duos have. They're as committed to the greater good as they are to their individual well-being.

## LARGER TEAMS

Whether it's building companies, writing books, recording albums, or making movies, a team is often behind major creative accomplishments. Behind the scenes of every success are a lot of people who make the accomplishments of the person in the spotlight possible.

*The Unmistakable Creative* podcast, the books I write, and all of the creative output of our company is a collaborative effort. None of it would be possible without the help of other people. While I might be the face and voice of *The Unmistakable Creative,* about a dozen people make the work possible:

- Guests offer their time to share their wisdom and insights with our listeners.

- Fans support our work by buying books, listening to the show, and sharing what we do.

- My business partner, Brian Koehn, and copywriter, Kingshuk Mukherjee, all keep things running smoothly.

- Mars Dorian, our special projects artist, adds an unmistakable signature to our work.

- My editor, Stephanie, has bet on my ability to produce a book and then edits it into the best possible version.

- My agent, Lisa, makes sure I get paid fairly, negotiates the best terms, and acts as my personal cheerleader.

- My writing coach, Robin, keeps me on track and pushes me forward on big creative projects.

Your team functions as a form of emotional support. When all you want to do is quit, a team encourages you to keep going. Numerous studies have shown that by going through difficult experiences together, the team forms a stronger bond. Y Combinator president Sam Altman says that they invest in only about one out of ten *solo* start-up founders: The failure rate for people working alone is simply too high.

The right partners and team members also enable you to accomplish far more. The quality and volume of my personal creative output improved significantly after we built a strong team. Shortly after we hired our content strategist Kingshuk Mukherjee, he increased the conversion rates on our website and the open rates on our newsletter. He also shaped our Sunday newsletter into what we had been attempting to create for two years: an interesting and fun to read collection of stories and ideas from around the internet.

In your own search for creative collaborators, it's important to understand your strengths and weaknesses (see Part Two, "Listening to Yourself"). The natural temptation is to partner with people who are just like you, but this is a recipe for disaster because you share the same weaknesses, and as a result those don't get addressed.

## OUR RELATIONSHIPS AND THEIR EFFECT ON CREATIVE ENERGY

One of the most important choices you make in your life is the people with whom you surround yourself. They can inspire and lift you up or they can sap your spirit and bring you down. Your network will determine your happiness, creativity, productivity, and even your net worth because the mind-set, beliefs, and behavior of the people you know will inevitably rub off on you.

Every person, situation, or circumstance has an energy. Some of these lower our own energy. When we tolerate something that's less than ideal or not to our liking, we tend to do so out of scarcity. And in many ways this is actually a lack of self-respect. We think it can't be better or there aren't many more options. This can start to become a huge energy drain, and at some point the effort isn't worth the potential reward.

After college, I remained in touch with two friends who had the superpower of taking any situation and seeing the worst in it. If you were dating someone new, they'd give you all the reasons it wasn't going to work out. If you got a new job, they'd tell you all the reasons you'd probably lose it.

Needless to say, it was emotionally exhausting to spend time with them, and it was turning me into a negative person. Eventually I had to cut ties with them.

"Negative people can increase our stress and hamper our ability to choose the positive. It is important to protect ourselves against negativity because it can have harsh effects on our bodies, leading to headaches, exhaustion, anxiety, and shortened life spans," says happiness researcher Michelle Gielan. Toxic relationships cut off the flow of creativity. They cause us to hold back out of fear, judgment, and disapproval. Their sound can be so deafening that we're unable to hear the voices of encouragement that have the potential to bring out the best in us.

My business partner, Brian, for example, is a perpetual optimist. If we take a hit financially in our business, he always seems to uncover ways of making more money than we might have lost. He is also quick to remind me that it can always be replaced.

If I find myself worrying, stressing, and feeling anxiety-ridden over anything, he manages to talk me out of it. He's able to see a bright future even in the darkest of times and to give people hope when things seem hopeless. Having Brian in my life has made me much more creative.

Or consider a documentary filmmaker friend who had a great idea for a stop-motion animation. Not only did she have zero animation knowledge, she had no drawing ability. What she did have, however, was Amy, her documentary film partner, who was the most upbeat, supportive person she knew. Her partner basically said "go for it," that her childlike drawings would work just fine, given the subject matter of the animation. So my friend took an animation class, did her own drawings, and a year later showed her film to a small group in her living room. When the credits rolled, one read "To Amy, the Queen of Encouragement."

When I asked Facebook friends whom they turn to for creative inspiration, many people mentioned their significant others. Rachel James, a musician and *Unmistakable Creative* listener, wrote:

> My husband and I are full-time musicians and we have projects together and separately. He has, in every way, made me a better musician, creator, performer, producer, and person. There is not a day that goes by that he doesn't whisper words of encouragement or challenge me to meet my fullest potential. This is the sort of partnership that I had always hoped for, but never experienced until the last 4 years with Dave. It is an incredible blessing.

## CONNECTION

One genuine connection will do far more for your creative practice than a thousand fans/friends on Facebook or a million followers on Twitter. What's the point of having a thousand friends if you can't pick up the phone and call one of them at two a.m.?

In fact, "Would this person come and bail me out of jail if I got arrested doing something stupid?" might be a perfect litmus test for the depth of your connection with someone.

The impact that a single connection can have on our lives and our creativity is dramatically apparent in the following story: While singing Journey cover songs at nightclubs in Manila, a young man was poor, nearly homeless. But with the encouragement and help of his best friend, he continually uploaded videos of himself to YouTube. The actual band Journey was looking for a singer, and guitarist Neal Schon contacted him and asked if he was interested in singing for the "real Journey." Today Arnel Pineda is Journey's lead singer.

Sometimes we'll connect with a purpose or in search of answers to whatever it is we're stuck on. Other times we simply need to hear another person's voice to stay inspired and motivated. For instance:

- When I've been blocked, or start to get really far off topic, I usually call my collaborator Robin for a pep talk and guidance on where to head next.

- When I don't feel inspired and just need someone to listen, I call my friend the memoirist Reema Zaman.

- On occasion I have a catch up call with other author friends to ask how they got past particularly difficult sections of a book or creative project.

○ Once a day, I check in with my business partner, not only to discuss business matters but to help each other maintain an optimistic state of mind.

In a world filled with digital tools that allow us to connect with anybody through a "follow" or "friend request," it's tempting to limit our contact with other people to the internet. But when we do that we miss out on opportunities for much deeper and more meaningful relationships.

In their book *How Google Works,* Jonathan Rosenberg and Eric Schmidt made the following observation:

Mervin Kelly, the late chairman of the board of Bell Labs, designed his company's buildings to promote interactions between employees. It was practically impossible for an engineer or scientist to walk down the long halls without running into a colleague or being pulled into an office. This sort of serendipitous encounter will never happen when you are working at home.

A group of engineers on different teams playing pool at the Googleplex created AdSense, a multibillion-dollar business. This is just one of the many Google products that have emerged from serendipitous encounters. While you don't have to build a personal Googleplex, it's tremendously important that you connect with people in person to fuel your creativity.

It's not a coincidence that the business partner I've had the most fruitful relationship with is also the one I see in person multiple times a week. Our copywriter, Kingshuk also lives in Southern California. It's a setup for serendipity. When our team gets together in person, our productivity and creativity seem to skyrocket. Each of our in-person meetings has led to new ideas for content, products, and the growth of our business.

## ANCHORS AND WINGS

At some point, you'll outgrow people. This is necessary for your progress and evolution. Those who are truly in your corner will understand and support you. The ones who are not will be filled with envy and regard your growth as bittersweet, and the foundation on which the relationship is built will be cracked and eventually shattered.

Often this tends to be revealed first in the darkest hours. It's easy to stand in someone's corner when they're kicking ass and taking names. But it's how you treat them when they're falling apart that determines true loyalty and support. Kick someone when they're down and that's how they'll remember you when they eventually rise again.

One of the simplest, most profound statements I've ever heard about support came from author Colin Wright, who said, "You want someone who gives you wings, not someone who is an anchor." It's often tempting to compromise on your values and change who you are in an effort to please another person, gain their approval, or meet their standards. In the process these people become anchors rather than giving us wings. Anchors keep ships from being able to move, and the same could be said for people like this in our lives. They stifle our growth and prevent us from being able to move.

In 2013, a partner and I who had worked together for two years decided it was time for us to part ways. We simply didn't have the same vision, values, enthusiasm, and commitment for what we wanted to create. Six months afterward, I had self-published *The Art of Being Unmistakable*, which became a *Wall Street Journal* bestseller; tickets for the Instigator Experience conference had sold out; and we had gone from $600 in the bank in June to $120,000 by January. While I learned quite a bit from him about design and typography, all of which came full circle when we rebranded as Unmistakable Creative, it was clear that by staying together we were holding each other back. When you release the people in your life who are anchors, you end up growing wings.

## WHERE IS YOUR COMMUNITY?

When my father arrived in Edmonton, Alberta, as a postdoctoral student, he didn't know anyone. My mother and I were still in India, due to arrive about six weeks later. A few years ago, one of my dad's friends from Edmonton was visiting and I asked how they got to know each other.

My dad had opened up the phone book, searched for "Telugu" people (the term for people from the Indian state of Andhra Pradesh), and called one of them. This random Telugu gentleman told my dad that everyone was out of town for a wedding, but invited him to a function the following week. The irony of the internet is that this would be much easier today, yet we'd probably think it was ludicrous if somebody reached out in this way.

By the time we left Edmonton in 1986, my parents had built a community of hundreds of friends, many of whom remain in their lives to this day. In four years of living in Canada, I recall only one or two weekends when we didn't have a party or function to go to. This was the first time I experienced a true community.

LISTEN TO: LIN-MANUEL MIRANDA

**My favorite thing is bringing the song into the room to my collaborators. That's my favorite part of the process. . . . It's the moment when I know my collaborators are going to make it better.**

Perhaps you're wondering what my dad's story has to do with creative practice. When immigrants arrive in a new country, they are effectively building a life from scratch. Even though they aren't making art per se, they are creating something from nothing, making a life they find rich, meaningful, and fulfilling.

In any creative endeavor it's helpful to be connected to people who are having a similar experience or have overcome the obstacles we might be struggling with. The Telugu community of Edmonton connected my father to people who had the shared experience of starting life in a new country known for its bone-chilling winters, where brown people and extreme weather are an unnatural combo.

While it's unlikely you'd open the phone book and start calling people of the same ethnicity in the year 2018, one thing still holds true: Joining a community is part of our evolution.

"We evolved as communities," said Jon Levy in an interview on *The Unmistakable Creative*:

> The concept of meeting people was a rare occurrence because we lived in these tribal groups for the majority of our early stage as a species. What made the community work was that there was joint activity. So when you look back at the people you bonded with the fastest it was probably because you had something to overcome together that you had to work together for.

My oldest friend from college is another example of the satisfaction to be found in creative community. Growing up immersed in traditional Indian dance, she has passed on her cultural heritage to her three daughters. "It brought great joy into [my mother's] life and she shared it with many others in our Southern California community," she says. "She never charged any money for teaching all the girls in the community, including my sister and me. We would move aside the furniture in the living room on weekends and our home would turn into a dance school. She organized hundreds of programs over the decades, and the community loved the way she brought everyone together and celebrated Bengali culture." Even though my friend documents her daughters' performances at *puja*s (an Indian religious ritual) and community/cultural programs in the form of photographs and videos, she doesn't do so for public consumption. All the links are kept private and selectively shared with her family members. "Having lost my mother at an early age, documenting and preserving treasured life experiences is really important to me. She has been gone now for almost seventeen years but the traditions remain strong. We teach our children the dances she taught us as children. Our children gain a strong sense of community, and Bengali music/dance becomes a part of their lives, too."

Communities support and amplify our creativity. They make us feel as if we're part of something greater than ourselves and enable us to have the confidence that we'll have someone to catch us when we inevitably fall.

Communities occur in many shapes and sizes. They can be in-person events like conferences and small dinners, or they can exist virtually as Facebook groups and online forums like Reddit. Communities give us a place to ask questions, to share our work, and to solicit feedback, all of which are essential for bringing forth our best creative work.

## IN-PERSON COMMUNITIES

We all need support in the creative process. What we do isn't easy. We spend hours on end in quiet rooms trying to create something of value for the world. But to call it "work" would seem like nonsense to many people. After all, we don't pull twelve-hour shifts and come home sleep-deprived. Often we're not even getting paid. We wander back and forth between our coffee makers and our desks. People seem to have no problem continually interrupting us to assist with their errands and minor needs because we're not performing surgery.

The actual work that goes into a book, a film, a piece of music, or a piece of art is often overlooked, or at least underappreciated, by those who don't make art. It's almost as if they assume that books on shelves at Barnes & Noble fall from the sky. They forget that somebody spent hours on end in a quiet room making whatever it is they're consuming.

As creatives, we exist in a separate world. It's as if we're part of a secret society whose members are the only ones who understand the nature of our work. "Artists are always misfits. Even when you plant them in artist colonies, they feel like misfits among misfits," says writer Heather Havrilesky. We have to find communities and support systems composed of people just like us, so we feel like we belong, at least a tiny bit.

In 2013, I was at a strange crossroads in my life and career. *The Unmistakable Creative* (at the time *BlogcastFM*) didn't quite have the traction that I wanted. A few months later, I stumbled upon AJ Leon and his band of Misfits. AJ invited me to speak at his first Misfit Conference, and two things happened that could have taken place only in person:

- I spent a significant amount of the weekend speaking with Greg Hartle, who would go on to become my mentor and play a major role in building what eventually became *Unmistakable Creative* and in planning the Instigator Experience.

○ AJ pulled me aside between drinks during the second night of the event and asked me why I was a behind-the-scenes person. At the time I was trying to find work managing social media for other creatives. He persuaded me to focus on my own creative work, which eventually resulted in my self-published book *The Art of Being Unmistakable*.

The right in-person encounter enabled me to find a mentor, gain confidence in my creative capabilities, and drastically change my life. Creative people gravitate toward one another. Being surrounded by other successful creatives begets more success in your own work. In-person communities can support and encourage your creative practice. They can provide accountability, push you beyond your comfort zones, and even stimulate new directions.

## CONFERENCES

Even in the age of the internet when we're more digitally connected than we've ever been, the conference business is booming. The truth is that virtual interactions can't make up for meeting face-to-face. Human touch releases a substance called oxytocin, which results in a stronger bond between people. This can't take place when an interaction is purely virtual. If you think about the people you are closest to, it's likely that you met them in person at some point or another. Conferences can be a great way to listen to and learn from others in the creative process.

The 99U Conference was born out of author Scott Belsky's company Bēhance. The event is described as a "one-of-a-kind live experience that inspires creative professionals to bring their ideas to life." Speakers have included design heads for major brands, well-known photographers, authors, visual artists, and many more. It's become a go-to destination for many creative professionals.

The Summit Series is another example of a network made up of successful people. In addition to several yearly events at a ski resort in Utah where venture capitalists, start-up founders, authors, and artists gather, they've held a flagship event called Summit at Sea. Described as a combination of Burning Man and TED, it draws celebrities like musician John Legend and actress Kristen Bell. In order to attend an event, you have to receive an invitation from someone else within the community.

Author and book consultant Linda Sivertsen hosts a writing retreat that takes place in Carmel, California. Participants are brought together for three days of writing and shaping their ideas. The upside of retreats is that they tend to be small, intimate, and intense. Because of this, participants receive highly personalized attention from the person running the retreat. Large volumes of creative expression result from multiple days of immersion. Many of the attendees at Sivertsen's retreats end up getting book deals. A retreat with the right person can be invaluable to your life and career, but it will likely also set you back a few thousand dollars.

## SUPPORT GROUPS

After Julia Cameron's book *The Artist's Way* came out, what she refers to as "creative clusters" formed. "Creative recovery at its best is a nonhierarchical, peer-run collective process," says Cameron. Being a member of this kind of group can help you find peers to bounce ideas off or gain insights from. In order for a group to be valuable, you want its members to be people who actually take action. It's easy to sit around and talk about creativity without actually creating anything and fool yourself into thinking you've done something productive. As Cameron says, "Creative clusters should be practiced through creative action, not theory."

If you can't find one, consider organizing your own creative support group. Invite three or four successful people who ideally don't know one another. If you do this on an ongoing basis, you'll find that not only does your network expand, but you'll also play a role in helping others. I know of an informal group that used to meet every other week to share their creative work. Called Fortnightly, it was made up of four to five couples who all lived in a suburban neighborhood but whose hearts remained in the East Village and Brooklyn. They included a doctor who oil-painted abstract works; a marketing executive who wrote short stories; the mother of six kids who was a poet; a machinist who sculpted wood; and an office manager/novelist. Knowing that they would be presenting to one another kept them motivated to carve out regular time for their creative expression. The commitment to meeting every other week became an integral part of their creative practice.

LISTEN TO: **MIKE BIRBIGLIA**

I met people whom I could bounce jokes and ideas off of. They'd give me candid feedback, and I tried to listen. I wasn't great at it at first. It's hard to hear criticism. But I've learned that harsh feedback, constructive feedback, even weird, random feedback, is all helpful, if you know the essence of what you're trying to convey.

## ACCOUNTABILITY

One of the challenges of creative work is that the work itself is often done in a vacuum without anybody holding us accountable. Nobody puts a gun to an author's head and forces him to write, and we're not going to get fired if we don't make our art today.

That's where the power of support groups and accountability comes in. "When we are answering to other people, we can do things we can't do on our own," says author Laura Vanderkam in an article on FastCompany.com.

When we're answering to another person, we suddenly feel more obligated to follow through on what we said we were going to do. Being negatively judged by another person can actually work to our advantage in certain scenarios. Just to avoid being labeled as flaky or unreliable we're much more likely to follow through.

But accountability goes far beyond just enabling us to follow through.

A person who holds us accountable can help us to overcome creative challenges and get unstuck when we're experiencing creative blocks. They can listen to our ideas, provide valuable feedback, and in some cases see what we don't.

They can also push us when they think we're capable of higher standards. When people hold us to higher standards, their feedback might initially sting, but what we have to realize is that they're trying to get our best work out of us.

If you saw some of the notes that get exchanged between an author and editor during the process of writing a book, you'd get to see exactly this happening.

During this exchange, what is actually accountability feels a bit more like a creative root canal. You have to keep reminding yourself that these people are on your side. You develop a thick skin and learn not to take comments personally.

When I got the first round of edits back on the manuscript for my previous book, my editor tried bribing me with a steak dinner to make the changes in a week. Given how much needed to be fixed, I ate the steak and told her it wouldn't be possible. But I did manage to turn it in about a week later. One of the many things that somehow two women and an Indian author had overlooked during the first draft was that I had too many white males as examples to back up my points. My editor was holding me accountable to the highest possible standard.

That's how accountability works sometimes. You might hate the process, but you'll love the result.

## FOOD FOR THOUGHT

We don't have to go too far outside of our own geography or even spend any money to connect with like-minded creatives. Tina Roth Eisenberg was craving more of what she experienced at the conferences she attended, connecting with people in person. But conferences are often expensive and not accessible to everyone. In her talk at the 99U Conference she quoted author Clay Shirky: "We overvalue access to information and undervalue access to each other."

So she created a monthly lecture series for the creative community in New York City that included breakfast and a twenty-minute talk. It quickly grew to the point where more than five hundred people were attending every month. After two years of running the series, Eisenberg was approached by people around the world about running "CreativeMornings" in their cities. Today CreativeMornings takes place in more than eighty cities and forty countries.

Food can be a powerful tool for building community. After all, we've been eating and drinking together since almost the beginning of our existence as a species. Meals also give us a level of intimacy that just isn't possible in a conference setting.

### The Influencers Dinner

Jon Levy, author of *The 2 AM Principle*, started a Manhattan series called the Influencers Dinner. At this invitation-only event, participants cook a meal together and are not allowed to talk about their careers until the meal is served. Former guests at the dinner have included professional athletes, successful entrepreneurs, artists, and many other high achievers. Some of the guests at a salon that Levy held in Los Angeles included a woman who owned the largest reality show casting agency in the world, a professional magician, a journalist who had interviewed people on MTV, and an author/professor who studied the science of humor.

### Midnight Brunch

Emily Cavalier created Midnight Brunch, which she describes as a "rogue dinner party that happens in the middle of the night, featuring exotic food and craft cocktails." It's a mash-up of the luxury and underground scenes, where participants meet trendsetters in the arts, media, and technology.

### Unmistakable Dinners

On occasion, our team at Unmistakable Creative will host intimate dinners where we bring together a group of our former guests and one or two of our listeners. And the conversation at the dinner table begins with questions like, "Share one confession and one crime that you've committed." It's always interesting to hear these kinds of stories from highly successful people.

## VIRTUAL COMMUNITIES

A virtual community usually lives on the internet (website, Facebook group/fan page, Slack channel, etc.) and centers around a shared interest, facilitating communication among members.

The upsides of virtual communities are that they are inexpensive or free, relatively easy to find, and accessible to almost anyone. It's also nearly effortless to ask questions and solicit feedback on your creative work.

The downsides of virtual communities are that you're one of many members and somewhat anonymous. It can be difficult to cut through the noise to get your questions answered or receive feedback. Because the conversation isn't face-to-face, members don't have a deep connection or a sense of accountability.

Virtual communities run the gamut. Some are open to everybody. Others are private and require an invitation or referral. Here are some virtual communities that are thriving:

- We have a private Unmistakable Creative Facebook group where our listeners can connect with other listeners, discuss episodes of the show, and meet potential creative collaborators. (See page 187 for more on this.)

- Author Scott Stratten runs a private Facebook group called Speak 'n Spill, where professional speakers can ask for advice, share tips, and connect with their peers.

○ Chris Guillebeau's annual event, the World Domination Summit, was born out of the virtual community based on his blog, *The Art of Non-Conformity.* In addition, a Facebook group allows attendees to stay in touch with one another after the event, and local World Domination Summit meet-ups are available.

Virtual communities can also serve as bridges between online and in-person relationships. In 2004, it wasn't as common as it is today to meet online friends in person. Yelp founders closed that gap by connecting people through food and drink without the pressures that often accompanied online dating. These communities, known as the "Yelp Elite," started popping up in multiple cities, and Yelp grew into one of the most popular websites on the internet for reviews of bars, restaurants, and other local establishments in cities around the world.

There's an online community for just about everything, which is great news for the purpose of creative practice. As I jokingly said about the Apple App Store, if you want to shoot an endangered species, there's probably an app for that. The same could be said for online communities. Whether you're a writer who wants to get feedback on something you've written, a visual artist who wants feedback on something you've drawn, or a musician who wants to share your music, an online community can serve as an important tool in your creative practice. And a good rule of thumb that people tend to forget is don't do anything online that you wouldn't do in person.

Support groups, virtual communities, conferences, intimate meals, and retreats all serve as fantastic tools to help us listen to and learn from others. They allow us not only to connect with like-minded creatives, but also to gain access to potential mentors and creative collaborators. Our most ambitious creative endeavors usually take a small army, and communities are a great way to begin seeking the people you want to have join yours.

## DELIBERATE CONSUMPTION AND CREATIVITY

We log in to Facebook, scroll through the news feed, and click away at whatever grabs our attention. We open up Netflix and search endlessly for the next TV show to binge-watch. For the most part, our consumption habits, the ways in which we take in information, are incredibly reactive. We might accidentally stumble on a creative spark or insight with this approach, but it's not a very reliable way to leverage others as a source of inspiration.

Deliberate consumption allows us, to quote the title of a book by Austin Kleon, to "steal like an artist." Everything we consume plants a potential seed for something we might create. We borrow ingredients from other people and create our own recipes and creative dishes. It's tempting to think of consumption solely in the form of various media formats. But deliberate consumption extends far beyond that. It can take the form of conversations with our close friends, visits to a museum, or even a short road trip. The point is that you are making a deliberate effort to take in information from the world around you.

Deliberate consumption is an essential ingredient for an effective creative practice. It gives us a reliable and repeatable way to let the work of others inform our own creative practice. It is to a creator what deliberate nutrition is to an athlete. In order to perform at his best, an athlete adopts a certain diet, which in turn improves his performance.

A creator must adopt certain consumption habits to produce his or her best work:

- You're not likely to produce an Oscar-winning film by watching cat videos on the internet.

- You're not going to write the great American novel by reading sensationalist clickbait.

- You won't learn to cook amazing meals from someone who considers warming up frozen food "cooking."

- You're not going to learn how to design a website or build an app from people who have never written a line of code in their lives.

- You don't want to take dance lessons from somebody who is an uncoordinated klutz.

The same way an athlete's performance would suffer by eating nothing but junk food, your creative capacity will suffer if you spend the overwhelming majority of your time consuming entertaining but ultimately useless content.

Two main ways to approach deliberate consumption are:

## THE PROCESS APPROACH

The actual content of what you're consuming doesn't matter as much as the fact that you follow a specific routine—a process—every day. For example, every morning before I start writing, I read for between thirty and forty-five minutes. The first words that I put down on paper are often from a quote, passage, or paragraph that I've underlined. This serves two main purposes:

1. It allows me to get something down on paper so I'm not faced with a daunting blank page.

2. It gives me a potential topic or prompt to riff on.

The process approach can be applied to any art form:

○ If you're a composer, listen to music or attend a concert that you love before you sit down to practice or play.

○ If you're a filmmaker, watch a movie or documentary.

○ If you're a visual artist, flip through the pages of an art book or visit a local museum.

- If you're a podcast host, listen to examples of great narrative journalism, such as NPR shows like *How I Built This, Serial,* or *This American Life.*

- If you have aspirations of becoming an amazing cook, dine at an amazing restaurant or read a book like *Kitchen Confidential* by Anthony Bourdain.

At its core, the process approach to deliberate consumption is simply setting aside a set amount of time for consuming the work of other people.

## THE CONTENT APPROACH

This approach to deliberate consumption tends to be driven by a particular area of interest that you have. I once spoke with Julien Smith, author and now CEO of a start-up called Breather, a bit like Airbnb for temporary office space, who said "I don't read blogs" even though he had one of the most popular blogs on the internet at the time. What he did read were obscure books about subjects like Japanese poetry. Julien's reading habits are exemplary of deliberate consumption. The effect of this approach? In his book *The Impact Equation,* which he cowrote with Chris Brogan, it's quite clear which sections Julien wrote and which sections Chris wrote. Deliberate consumption resulted in an incredibly distinctive voice.

Creator of iconic comedies such as *Superbad, Knocked Up,* and *The 40-Year-Old Virgin*, Judd Apatow obsessively consumed stand-up comedy as a high school student. While working for a high school radio show, he began interviewing famous comedians like Jerry Seinfeld and Steve Martin. Apatow's deliberate consumption habits led to an unmistakable brand of humor that has resulted in a thriving career.

Another spin on the content approach is to deliberately *diversify* your consumption habits. I highly recommend diversification if you're looking to stretch your creative capacity and develop a distinctive voice. As a writer primarily of prescriptive and social science–based nonfiction, I mostly read autobiographies, essay collections, and a bit of fiction. Some of my favorite books that have fallen out of the pattern of what I typically read include *A People's History of the United States,* Jhumpa Lahiri's *The Namesake,* and *Michael Jordan: The Life.*

"Authentic listening is simply the giving of our undivided attention to another without imposing our personal agendas, something that might take practice," says Kathryn Woodward, author of *Calling in "The One": 7 Weeks to Attract the Love of Your Life.* This is at the heart of what it means to listen to others. By opening ourselves to the ideas of others, we learn, grow, and evolve in creative practice.

Listening to others is transformative to the creative process because it opens our minds and our hearts. We learn the lessons that others impart to us and receive the gifts they give. We grow into better versions of ourselves and our creative practice evolves. When we cultivate a capacity to authentically listen, the return on investment is something that can last a lifetime. As David Bowie said:

I suppose for me as an artist it wasn't always just about expressing my work; I really wanted, more than anything else, to contribute in some way to the culture that I was living in.

In the end, isn't that what a creative practice, a creative life, is all about?

LISTEN TO: ANDY WARHOL

**Don't think about making art, just get it done. Let everyone else decide if it's good or bad, whether they love it or hate it. While they are deciding, make even more art.**

# UNMISTAKABLE PRACTICE:
## ACTIVITIES AND EXERCISES

### LISTENING TEAM

To become an unmistakable creative, you need a band of brothers and sisters to cheer you on, to give you feedback when you want it but not when you don't, to be your creative family. The first step in creating such a team of unpaid volunteers—your Listening Team—is to list all the people who already populate your life.

Write down everyone you interact with on at least a monthly basis. Don't stop to think about them, don't try to prioritize them, just get a list on paper. They can include family, friends, coworkers, teachers, club members, coffee shop acquaintances, your favorite bartender or personal trainer.

Okay, so now you have a pool of candidates for your Listening Team. Go down the list slowly and ask yourself: Does this person really hear me? Does this person make me feel energized, hopeful, confident, creative, smart, and appreciated? Does this person make me feel drained, second-guessed, negative, clumsy, and unsuccessful? It's possible that some people are neither one nor the other but instead a neutral presence for you. That's fine, just note it.

Now mark each name with one of the following:

1. **Loudmouth:** a king or queen of encouragement

2. **Off-key:** always a naysayer and master of the put-down

3. **No voice:** neither positive nor negative

Obviously, you want to recruit the Loudmouths for your Listening Team. Ideally you'll have five or six team members you can turn to for creative support, but even one or two is better than none. Once you've identified your Listening Team, try to make contact with them regularly. Maybe you'll have an actual meeting once a month. Maybe you'll do a check-in via text every morning. The important point is to integrate your team into your creative practice somehow.

## THE UNBOOK CLUB

Instead of starting a conventional book club, try listening to others . . . literally. Invite a group of people—the more diverse, the better—to meet regularly and discuss a podcast. Members take turns choosing the podcast, hosting the gathering, and asking the group specific questions about each podcast. You could organize a podcast club around a theme (time and art), a genre (graphic design), an issue (overcoming creative blocks), or simply concentrate on one particular podcast series. For more guidance, check out readers' discussion guides for book clubs—and then get creative.

You could base the whole club on Unmistakable Creative guests, for example. In the Unmistakable Creative Facebook group, listeners are able to connect with one another to discuss recent episodes, discover books, and talk about their own creative projects. One of our listeners, Milena Rangelov, even writes in-depth summaries of our episodes with key takeaways from each episode. Every couple of weeks we also ask our listeners to share something they've made or whatever they're working on. To learn more about the Unmistakable Creative Facebook group, visit www.facebook.com/groups/831215510267204.

## IN-DEPTH LISTENING

Our day-to-day consumption of information tends to be scattered, superficial, and inconsistent—not a great recipe for our creative soup. I challenge you to find a subject you can sink your teeth into, scouring every possible resource until you've become an expert. It doesn't matter whether it's another artist, a historical period, an esoteric branch of physics, or the cuisine of the Middle East. The point is to immerse yourself in one carefully defined area, to listen to everything ever written, said, or created about that subject.

This exercise serves a couple of purposes. First, it's simply a great way to keep your brain in shape by stretching it in new directions. And the more robust your brain, the more robust your creative muscle will be. But a more subtle benefit is that all that focus will inevitably inform your creative expression. It may not be as obvious as learning Italian so you can write Italian sonnets. Perhaps it will be more like seeing a forest differently as you photograph it because you've been studying the industrial revolution or how paper is made.

One friend, whose main creative expression is jewelry design, chooses a new endeavor every year. In the last twelve years, she's learned metal welding, tai chi, scuba diving, how to make nut brittles with various herbs and spices, and knitting, among other things. You don't have to take a year—but it is good to give yourself a time frame. Depending on the breadth of your study, it could be a month or more.

PART FIVE

# NOT
# A
# CONCLUSION

When you take your final breath, what will you leave behind? Will there be anything for people to remember you by? Projects, art, and connections that tell your story? Will the world be more interesting for your having been here? Or will there simply be a generic obituary somewhere on the internet?

We underestimate what we could do in a year but overestimate what we could do in a day. Our day-to-day effort doesn't yield obvious, instant results, so we tend to undervalue it. But it's daily effort that ultimately leads to the realization of any creative dream or goal. Regardless of your age, with a daily creative practice, creative possibilities become infinite.

If you commit to a lifetime of creative practice—"everything you create, contribute, affect and impact" and "the personal legacy you leave at the end of your life, including all the tangible and intangible things you've created"—you'll build what author and speaker Pamela Slim describes as a body of work. You'll experience the joy, the tangible and intangible rewards of an ongoing creative practice. You'll establish a personal creative legacy.

In Japan, there's a term known as *ikigai*, which means a reason to get up in the morning. People of Okinawa are believed to be the longest lived people in the world because they have *ikigai*. When we live a creative life every day over the course of a lifetime, it gives us not only a reason to get up in the morning, but something to look forward to. By designing just one small part of our day, we become deliberate creators of our life experience. When we make art every day, and listen to our creativity, we have a reason to get up in the morning. We have *ikigai*.

So make art every day. Make it through good times and bad times. Make it when you're consumed by grief and overwhelmed with joy. Make it because the process brings you joy.

Creative work is a daily journey. It's filled with false starts, detours, dead ends, missed connections, and false horizons. It leads you down unexpected roads and to unimagined destinations. It will challenge, inspire, and provoke you. It will push you to your limits and enable you to exceed those limits. Creative work changes its creator as much as if not more than the audience it collides with. To listen to creativity is to take this journey, seek out this change, and evolve into the next best version of ourselves.

# A PORTFOLIO OF EXPERIENCES THAT ADD MEANING TO OUR LIVES

For two years my creative life had been defined by the process of writing books. With this book coming to a close, I had to find something to fill the void. I found myself returning to music. I went to my local Guitar Center and purchased a guitar. Fortunately a guitar is cheaper and more versatile than a tuba. If I had any aspirations to serenade some woman in my life, a guitar would be much more effective. It was as if my listening journey that began with Michael Jackson had come full circle. I was very much a beginner again and was forced to listen closely to every note and every chord.

As I was walking on the beach with our content strategist and copywriter, Kingshuk, he said something that really struck me.

"When you have these outlets for your creativity—surfing, snowboarding, playing the guitar—if something else in your life isn't going well, you still have these activities that bring you a great deal of joy. Those guys on Wall Street who kill themselves when the market crashes, I'm convinced it's because their identity is wrapped up in just one thing, their work."

Our ongoing expression of creativity in multiple forms—music, cooking, visual art, writing, woodworking—allows us to build a portfolio of meaningful experiences that don't depend on any one person or thing that's out of our control for our happiness and fulfillment. It enables us to tune in and listen to whatever it is we have a desire to express.

# ACT IN ANTICIPATION AND LISTEN EVERY DAY

When I was preparing to write this book, I used many of the habits I've described to get in creative shape. But weeks went by and I couldn't get a handle on where to begin. Finally, one day I left my desk and the pile of reference material I had accumulated to go for a walk around the neighborhood (see page 141). I emptied my mind and observed: unusual seed pods dangling from a tree I had never noticed before; seven wild turkeys trotting across a lawn; wind chimes; and finally, a labyrinth made of stones. At some point in the middle of that walk, the idea of listening as a gateway to creativity sprang to life. I just had to have faith in my creative practice.

Writing this book forced me not only to examine, but to become hyperaware of my own habits. It's made me realize that I have many of the same flaws that everyone else has when it comes to getting distracted and making no progress with creative work. I waste time online, fall asleep with my laptop in my bed, and do many of the other things that I've recommended you avoid. But this is more the exception than the norm.

These habits, hacks, rituals, and routines that I've suggested are microinterventions to help you with your creativity. None of them will turn you into a creative superstar overnight. Instead, the cumulative effect of creative habits over a long enough time line is pure joy that comes from your full self-expression. You'll find a depth, significance, and purpose that can be accessed only when your creative expression becomes a daily lifelong practice.

At the end of a yoga class, after the final pose known as Savasana, instructors ask students to assume a fetal position before returning to sitting with their hands at heart center. The fetal position symbolizes rebirth, a perfect metaphor for our creative practice. With each day of practice we are reborn with the knowledge, experience, and insights we gain. We become more attuned to our ability to listen to our creativity, ourselves, our environment, and others. We approach our art, whether that is a blank page, a canvas, a camera, an instrument, or even an app we're building, having grown and evolved into the next best version of ourselves.

So listen to your environments. Listen to others.

Then let go of all that, silence it.

What you'll hear is that singular creative voice welling up out of the stillness. We all have it.

Listen.

Can you hear it?

# ACKNOWLEDGMENTS

Every book is the result of a team whose work takes place behind the scenes, who make invaluable contributions, who de-
serve far more than an acknowledgements page, and who
ultimately make the job of any author possible.

Stephanie Frerich, thank you for believing in my work and my
ideas, and for taking a chance on me.

Vivian Roberson, thank you for your commitment to such
high editorial standards.

Robin Dellabough, thank you for pushing me, challenging
me, being tough on me, and supporting me through every ob-
stacle I faced in writing this book. You've been a coach, a mentor, a friend, and an amazing collaborator. Working with you on
this project, and my previous book, has been one of the great
gifts of my life.

Lisa Dimona, you've helped me do more than write a book.

You've helped me start one of the most important chapters of my life.

Brian Koehn, thank you for sticking it out, through good times and bad times, when every conceivable metric said we should quit. You've been an amazing business partner and an even better friend.

To Kingshuk Mukherjee, thank you for challenging me to make every expression of my creativity unmistakable.

Tom Nielsen and the Brightsight group, thank you for giving me stages to help spread these ideas to thousands of people.

Charmaine Haworth, thank you for teaching me what it truly means to design a beautiful environment that unleashes creativity.

To the hundreds of guests and thousands of listeners around the world who make *The Unmistakable Creative* podcast what it is, none of this would be possible without your generosity and support.

# RESOURCES

## APPS

Boomerang for email
Flipd
Focus
Focus@Will
Full-screen mode on all apps
Google Calendar for time management
MacJournal
News Feed Eradicator
Oblique Strategies
RescueTime
Scrivener
Unroll.Me

## BLOGS AND WEBSITES

https://conference.99u.com
www.diamandis.com/blog/topic/abundance-insider

https://makesomething365.blogspot.com

http://karenkavett.com/blog/3555/dont-break-the-chain-calendar-2017
    -free-motivational-tool-printable.php

www.eatthis.com/clean-eating-plan

## BOOKS

Carrie Barron and Alton Barron, *The Creativity Cure: How to Build Happiness with Your Own Two Hands*

Todd Brison, *The Creative's Curse*

Julia Cameron, *The Artist's Way: A Spiritual Path to Higher Creativity*

Julia Cameron, *Walking in This World: The Practical Art of Creativity*

Shelley Carson, *Your Creative Brain: Seven Steps to Maximize Imagination, Productivity, and Innovation in Your Life*

Mason Currey, *Daily Rituals: How Artists Work*

Jane Davies, *Collage Journeys: A Practical Guide to Creating Personal Artwork*

Elizabeth Gilbert, *Big Magic: Creative Living Beyond Fear*

Arianna Huffington, *The Sleep Revolution: Transforming Your Life, One Night at a Time*

Tami Lynn Kent, *Wild Creative: Igniting Your Passion and Potential in Work, Home, and Life*

Marie Kondo, *The Life-Changing Magic of Tidying Up: The Japanese Art of Decluttering and Organizing*

Jonah Lehrer, *Imagine: How Creativity Works*

Alex Soojung-Kim Pang, *Rest: Why You Get More Done When You Work Less*

Andrea Pippins, *Becoming Me: A Work in Progress: Color, Journal & Brainstorm Your Way to a Creative Life*

SARK, *Make Your Creative Dreams Real: A Plan for Procrastinators, Perfectionists, Busy People, and People Who Would Really Rather Sleep All Day*

Noah Scalin, *Unstuck: 52 Ways to Get (and Keep) Your Creativity Flowing at Home, at Work & in Your Studio*

Joshua Wolf Shenk, *Powers of Two: How Relationships Drive Creativity*

Twyla Tharp, *The Creative Habit: Learn It and Use It for Life*

Florence Williams, *The Nature Fix: Why Nature Makes Us Happier, Health-ier, and More Creative*

Declan Wilson, *The Millennial Way: Step Up, Step Out, Step Forward*

Susan G. Wooldridge, *Foolsgold: Making Something from Nothing and Freeing Your Creative Process*

## AUDIOBOOKS

Walter Isaacson, *Steve Jobs*

Shonda Rhimes, *Year of Yes: How to Dance It Out, Stand in the Sun and Be Your Own Person*

Alice Schroeder, *The Snowball: Warren Buffett and the Business of Life*

Ashlee Vance, *Elon Musk: Tesla, SpaceX, and the Quest for a Fantastic Future*

# INDEX

*Abundance: The Future Is Better Than You Think* (Diamandis), 109
*Abundance Insider,* 111
Accidental Creative, 66
accountability, 174–76
Achor, Shawn, 118
activation energy, 118–25
  creativity and, 120–21
  deliberate practice, 121–25
  distraction and, 118–20
activities and exercises, 15–16, 67–77, 143–47, 186–89
  autobiography, 73–75
  childhood creativity, 72–73
  cross-training, 147
  dreams, 71–72
  genogram, 75–77
  in-depth listening, 188–89
  Listening Team, 186–87
  make something every day, 145–46

  music, 143
  playdates, 144–45
  seven times three meditation, 143–44
  social fasting, 146–47
  unbook club, 187–88
  "What would happen if," 67–71
ADHD, 92
AdSense, 164
advice, 39–40
Affleck, Ben, 155–56
Altman, Sam, 159
Amabile, Teresa, 32
Amazon, 25
ambient noise, 95
analog vs. digital work methods, 106–9
anchors vs. wings, people as, 165–66
Angelou, Maya, 42
anxiety, 107–8
Anxiety.org, 108
Apatow, Judd, 183–84

# Index

Apple, 52–53

apps and products, habit-forming, 99–111, 108

*Artist's Way, The* (Cameron), 9, 10, 51, 144, 145, 173

"Artist's Way in an Age of Self-Promotion, The" (Battan), 9–10

*Art of Being Unmistakable, The* (Rao), 25, 166, 171, 175

*Art of Non-Conformity, The,* 179

art therapy, 29

*At All Costs,* 122–23

attachments, 21

attention, 127–28, 131

   residue, 102

   *see also* distractions; presence

Audible, 111

audience of one, creating for, 3–10, 48

   author's path to, 10–12

autobiography, creative, 73–75

Bajaj, Karan, 19–20

Battan, Carrie, 9–10

Baumeister, Roy, 113

Beck, Glenn, 25

Beethoven, Ludwig van, 53

*Before I Die,* 55

Bēhance, 172

Bell, Kristen, 172

Bell Labs, 164

Belsky, Scott, 172

*Be More with Less,* 84

Birbiglia, Mike, 174

*BlogcastFM,* 41, 42, 170

Bloomberg, Michael, 46

*Bloomberg by Bloomberg* (Bloomberg), 46

body, 55–66

   nutrition, 60–62

   sleep, *see* sleep

Bourdain, Anthony, 183

Bowie, David, 1–3, 28, 30, 184–85

Bowman, Gene, 61

Boykin, Jennifer, 8

brain, 33, 62, 112, 188–89

   exercise and, 63

   flow and, 124

   internet and, 100–104, 146–47

   music and, 93–94

   power questions and, 87–88

   sleep and, 56–57, 59, 71

   travel and, 140–41

   water and, 95–96

*Brain Pickings,* 7

Breather, 183

Brogan, Chris, 183

Brown, Brené, 33

Bunch, Jim, 81, 89, 102

Cameron, James, 60

Cameron, Julia, 9, 10, 47, 51, 144, 145, 173

Carr, Nicholas, 102–3

Carver, Courtney, 84

Cavalier, Emily, 177

certainty anchor, 112

chain method, 134

challenge/skills ratio, 129–30

Chang, Candy, 55

Chapman, Sandra Bond, 138

Chappelle, Dave, 131

Clear, James, 62, 117–18

clothing, 82, 84, 88, 113, 142

clutter, 83–84, 86

Coachella, 7

Colvin, Geoff, 121, 155

community, *see* connection, support, and community

comparison, 8–9, 11, 108, 111

conferences, 171–73, 176

connection, support, and community, 154–80

  accountability and, 174–76

  anchors and wings in, 165–66

  conferences, 171–73, 176

  energy and, 160–62

  food and, 176–77

  in-person communities, 169–77

  partnerships, 155–58

  support groups, 173–74

  teams, 158–60

  virtual communities, 178–80

Conradt, Stacy, 60

cortisol, 92, 94

creative clusters, 173

CreativeMornings, 176

creativity and creating, 16, 25, 33

  for audience of one, 3–10, 48

  for audience of one, author's path to, 10–12

  listening to, 14, 17–34

  outcomes in, 6–10

  paradox of, 3

  productivity and, 32–34

  regular practice of, 3–4

  separating results from effort in, 4–5

Csikszentmihalyi, Mihaly, 129, 133

curiosity, 53–55, 92, 137

Currey, Mason, 116

Cutts, Matt, 54, 55

Daft Punk, 6–7

*Daily Rituals: How Artists Work* (Currey), 116

Damon, Matt, 155–56

decision fatigue, 105, 112–14

deep work, 126, 134

*Deep Work* (Newport), 100

Delany, Mary, 45

deliberate consumption, 180–85

  content approach to, 183–85

  process approach to, 182–83

deliberate practice, 121–25

Dellabough, Robin, 125, 159, 163

DiAlto, Elizabeth, 153

Diamandis, Peter, 109, 111, 151

digital vs. analog work methods, 106–9

distractions, 101–3, 108, 109, 196

  activation energy and, 118–20

  dopamine and, 98–99

  eliminating and managing, 104–9

doer/dreamer partnerships, 157

dopamine, 94, 98–99, 107, 108, 130

Dorian, Mars, 158

dreamer/doer partnerships, 157

dreams and the subconscious mind, 59–60, 71–72

Duhigg, Charles, 107

Dweck, Carol, 21

Dylan, Bob, 26

effort

  measuring, 133–34

  results and, 4–5

ego, 21, 115, 152, 157–58

Eisenberg, Tina Roth, 176

email, 49, 98–99, 101, 103, 104, 106, 127, 128, 146
energy, 55–56
    relationships and, 160–62
England, Angela, 94
Eno, Brian, 2
environment, listening to, 14, 79–147
Ericsson, Anders, 121–22
Ernst, Michael, 95
exercise and physical activity, 63–66, 116, 117–18
exercises, *see* activities and exercises
expectations
    of others, 2, 3, 21
    of ourselves, 5, 137
extrinsic motivators, 7–8, 26–27

Fabian, Erik, 52
Facebook, 82, 98–99, 103, 106, 108, 128, 146, 162, 180
    groups, 169, 178, 179
    News Feed Eradicator, 106
    *see also* social media
family tree (genogram), 75–77
FastCompany.com, 174
feedback, 174–75, 179, 186
    immediate, 132–33
Ferguson, Brian, 64
Fields, Jonathan, 112
fixed mind-set, 21–22
Flipd, 119–20
flow, 33–34, 124, 126–38
    challenge/skills ratio and, 129–30
    effort measurement and, 133–34
    goals and feedback and, 132–33

interruptions and, 131–32
    passion and, 134–38
    time and, 130–31
    triggers of, 127–38
Focus, 105, 118
focus, 127–28
Focus@Will, 94, 132
food
    community and, 176–77
    nutrition, 60–62
forest, walking in, 91–92
Fortnightly, 173–74
*Four Agreements, The* (Ruiz), 87

Gaiman, Neil, 137
Gebben, Michael, 110
genius myth, 155
genogram, 75–77
Gershwin, George, 116
Gielan, Michelle, 161
Gladwell, Malcolm, 121
Glass, Ira, 57
Glei, Jocelyn, 101
goals
    clear, 132–33
    reminders of, 87
Godin, Seth, 34
Goodkin, Joe, 64
*Good Will Hunting*, 155
Google, 54, 99, 131, 164
Google Chrome, 128
Googleplex, 164
Grant, Adam, 4
*Groundhog Day*, 114
growth mind-set, 21
Guillebeau, Chris, 179

habits, 16, 111–12, 116–18, 196
  apps and products and, 99–111, 108
  focus and, 127
happiness, 20, 22, 27–31, 34, 126, 134
  flow and, 33–34
Hardy, Benjamin, 139
Hartle, Greg, 170–71
Havrilesky, Heather, 170
Haworth, Charmaine, 85
headphones, noise cancellation,
  96–97, 132
Hemingway, Ernest, 53
Henry, Todd, 44, 66
Hogshead, Sally, 38, 130
Holiday, Ryan, 4–5, 26, 95
"How Art Changes Your Brain" study, 29
How Google Works (Rosenberg and
  Schmidt), 164
Huffington, Arianna, 56, 57

ikigai, 194
Impact Equation, The (Brogan and Smith), 183
Influencers Dinner, 177
Insight Out (Seelig), 54
Instagram, 99, 103, 106, 128, 146
  see also social media
Instant Information Systems, 24
Instigator Experience, 75, 166, 171
internet, 6, 22, 49, 97–98, 100, 126, 127, 131,
  164, 167, 171
  brain and, 100–104, 146–47
  communities on, 178–80
  see also social media
interruptions, 131–32
  see also distractions
Intuit, 45–46

Jackson, Michael, 13, 195
Jackson-Cartwright, Parker, 122–23
Jacobs, David, 63
Jacobs, Tom, 28
James, Rachel, 162
Jobs, Steve, 91, 113
Jones, Sam, 155
Jordan, Michael, 156
Journal of Consumer Research, 95
journals, notebooks, and sketchbooks,
  51–53, 60, 106
Journey, 163

Kelly, Kevin, 100–101
Kelly, Mervin, 164
Kent, Tami Lynn, 91
Kickstarter, 41
Kitchen Confidential (Bourdain), 183
Kleon, Austin, 180
Knausgaard, Karl Ove, 124
Koehn, Brian (business partner), 104, 151,
  158, 161, 164–65
Kondo, Marie, 82, 85
Kotler, Steven, 94, 95, 126

Lady Gaga, 34
Lahiri, Jhumpa, 184
Lamott, Anne, 16
LaPorte, Danielle, 153
Legend, John, 172
Lehrer, Jonah, 26
L'Engle, Madeleine, 25
Leon, AJ, 40–41, 64, 170, 171
Levitin, Daniel, 86
Levy, Jon, 141, 168, 177
Life After Tampons, 8

*Life and Times of a Remarkable Misfit, The*
    (Leon), 41
*Life-Changing Magic of Tidying Up, The*
    (Kondo), 82, 85
listening, 13, 196–97
    to creativity, 14, 17–34
    to environment, 14, 79–147
    in-depth, 188–89
    to others, 15, 149–89
    to your body, 55–66
    to yourself, 14, 35–77, 127
Listening Team, 186–87
lone creator myth, 155
*Louder Than Words* (Henry), 44

Mah, Cheri, 57
Mantel, Hilary, 49
Martin, Steve, 184
measuring your effort, 133–34
Mediabistro, 24
meditation, 29, 50
    seven times three, 143–44
*Medium,* 48, 100
MentalFloss.com, 60
    clutter, 83–84, 86
*Michael Jordan: The Life* (Lazenby), 184
Midnight Brunch, 177
Millburn, Joshua Fields, 84
Mindfulness Based Art Therapy
    (MBAT), 29
*Minimalism: A Documentary About the
    Important Things,* 84
Miranda, Lin-Manuel, 167
Misfit Conference, 170
Monroe, Matt, 81
Moodley, Nisha, 41

Mukherjee, Kingshuk, 22–23, 117, 158, 159,
    165, 195
Mullis, Kary, 91
Murakami, Haruki, 12, 64
music
    listening to, 93–94, 143
    making, 21, 123–26, 132–33, 195

*Namesake, The* (Lahiri), 184
nature, 90–93, 133
*Nature Fix, The* (Williams), 91–92
negativity and toxic relationships, 109–10,
    142, 160–61
*Neurology,* 61, 63
Newport, Cal, 100, 101, 134
News Feed Eradicator, 106
*New Yorker,* 9
*New York Times,* 26
Nichols, Wallace, 95–96
Nicodemus, Ryan, 84
99U Conference, 172, 176
noise cancellation headphones, 96–97, 132
norepinephrine, 94
notebooks, journals, and sketchbooks,
    51–53, 60, 106
NPR, 183
nutrition, 60–62

Obama, Barack, 113
*Off Camera,* 155
Okinawa, 194
OneTab, 128
*Organized Mind, The* (Levitin), 86
*Originals: How Non-Conformists Move the
    World* (Grant), 4
oxytocin, 94, 171

*Pacific Standard,* 28
Pandora, 94
Pang, Alex Soojung-Kim, 56–57
*Paper Garden, The: An Artist Begins Her Life's Work at 72* (Peacock), 45
partnerships, 155–58
passion, 65, 134–38
Pavlov, Ivan, 88
Peacock, Molly, 45, 65
*Peak: Secrets from the New Science of Expertise* (Ericsson), 122
Peck, Sarah, 51–52
Pennebaker, James, 31
*People's History of the United States, A* (Zinn), 184
Perch Urbio, 86
perfectionism, 65
phones, 48, 58, 103, 104–5, 118–20
physical activity and exercise, 63–66, 116, 117–18
physical space, 83–97, 128–29
    clutter in, 83–84, 86
    creating your best space, 85–88
    nature, 90–93, 133
    noise in, 95, 96
    sound in, *see* sound environment
    tolerations in, 88–90
    water in, 95–96
Picasso, Pablo, 53
Pillay, Srinivasan, 92
Pineda, Arnel, 163
podcasts, 20–21, 109, 110
    club for discussing, 187–88
    *see also Unmistakable Creative* podcasts and guests

Popova, Maria, 7–8
    clutter, 83–84, 86
*PostSecret,* 24
Powell, Julie, 145
*Powers of Two* (Shenk), 157
*Practicing Mind, The* (Sterner), 47
presence, 45–48, 99, 103, 107
    judgment and, 47–48
*Presentation Zen* (Reynolds), 52–53
Pressfield, Steven, 39, 49, 116
Prevention.com, 59
    consumption and, 182–83
    rewards vs., 4–5, 20–25
procrastination, 49
productivity, 32–34, 127
    sleep and, 56
*Progress Principle, The* (Amabile), 32
Project 333, 84

Rangelov, Milena, 188
reading, 50–51, 103, 106, 126, 183, 184
Reddit, 169
relationships
    energy and, 160–62
    outgrowing, 165–66
    toxic, 109–10, 142, 160–61
    *see also* connection, support, and community
RescueTime, 105, 118, 146
resistance, 49–50
*Rest: Why You Get More Done When You Work Less* (Pang), 56–57
results and rewards, 16, 20, 34
    "making it," 25–27
    process and effort vs., 4–5, 20–25
retreats, 172–73

Reynolds, Garr, 52–53
Rilke, Rainer Maria, 135
rituals, 111–16, 196
    decision fatigue and,
        112–14
    habits, 116–18
    space and, 114–15
    timing and, 115–16
Rivera, Geraldo, 42
Robbins, Tony, 87
Rose, Darya Prno, 61, 62
Rosenberg, Jonathan, 164
Ruiz, Don Miguel, 87

Scalin, Noah, 145
Schmidt, Eric, 164
Schon, Neal, 163
*Scientific American*, 63
Scudamore, Brian, 48
Seelig, Tina, 54, 137
Seinfeld, Jerry, 134, 184
self-care, 28–29, 56
serotonin, 94
*Shallows, The: What the Internet Is Doing to
    Our Brains* (Carr), 102–3
shallow work, 126–27
Shapiro, Dani, 22, 51, 136, 152
Shenk, Joshua Wolf, 157
Shirky, Clay, 176
Shockey, Sarah Joy, 27
Silvia, Paul, 27–28
Sinek, Simon, 40
Singularity University, 151
Sivertsen, Linda, 172
sketchbooks, notebooks, and journals,
    51–53, 60, 106

skill level, 57, 123
    challenge and, 129–30
*Skimm, The*, 156
sleep, 56–58, 61
    dreams, 59–60, 71–72
    exercise and, 63
    tips for, 58–59
*Sleep Revolution, The* (Huffington), 56
Slim, Pamela, 137, 194
*Smarter Faster Better* (Duhigg), 107
smartphones, 48, 58, 103, 104–5,
    118–20
Smith, Julien, 183
social media, 6, 49, 100, 103–4, 106, 108,
    127, 128
    dopamine and, 98–99
    Facebook, *see* Facebook
    fasting experiment, 146–47
    Instagram, 99, 103, 106, 128, 146
    Twitter, 99, 103, 106, 128, 146, 162
solitude, solitary activities, 48–53
    journals, notebooks, and sketchbooks,
        51–53, 60, 106
    meditation, *see* meditation
    physical activities, 65
    reading, 50–51, 103, 106, 126, 183, 184
sound environment, 93–97
    music, 93–94, 143
    noise, 95, 96
space, physical, 83–97, 128–29
Speak 'n Spill, 178
Springer, Jerry, 42
Stanford Sleep Disorders Clinic, 57–58
*Stealing Fire* (Kotler and Wheal), 94
*Steal Like an Artist* (Kleon), 180
Sterner, Thomas, 47

*Still Writing: The Perils and Pleasures of a Creative Life* (Shapiro), 22, 136, 152
Stratten, Scott, 178
success, *see* results and rewards
*Summer of Amit,* 135–36
Summit at Sea, 172
Summit Series, 172
support, *see* connection, support, and community
surfing, 90–93, 104, 129, 133, 154, 195

teams, 158–60
    two-person, 155–58
tech environment, 97–111
    email, 49, 98–99, 101, 103, 104, 106, 127, 128, 146
    phones, 48, 58, 103, 104–5, 118–20
    *see also* internet
*Terminator, The,* 60
Tharp, Twyla, 53, 64, 123
thirty-day challenges, 54–55, 145
Tierney, John, 113
time, flow of, 130–31
timing, 115–16
to-do list, 128
tolerations, 88–90
toxic relationships, 109–10, 142, 160–61
Tracy, Brian, 104
trauma, healing from, 30–31
TurboTax, 45
*Turning Pro* (Pressfield), 39
Twitter, 99, 103, 106, 128, 146, 162
    *see also* social media
*2 AM Principle, The: Discover the Science of Adventure* (Levy), 141, 177

Uhls, Yalda, 108
Ultimate Game of Life, 81
unbook club, 187–88
University of North Carolina at Greensboro, 27–28
Unmistakable Creative, 22–23, 43, 44, 166
    dinners hosted by, 177
    Facebook group, 178, 187–88
*Unmistakable Creative* podcast and guests, 13, 15, 26, 38, 40–43, 47, 64, 81, 82, 95, 101, 104, 110, 117, 128, 130, 140, 141, 158, 162, 168, 171, 177, 187–88
    as *BlogcastFM,* 41, 42, 170
Unroll.Me, 109
*Unsubscribe: How to Kill Email Anxiety, Avoid Distractions, and Get Real Work Done* (Glei), 101
Untrained Housewife, 94

validation, 8, 11, 21, 37–38
    *see also* results and rewards
values, 38, 40
    listening to, 39–44
    uncovering, 43–44
Vanderkam, Laura, 174
Vanderveen, Dave, 141
van Gogh, Vincent, 53
virtual communities, 178–80

Wahl, Erik, 64
*Wall Street Journal,* 166
Warhol, Andy, 185
Warren, Frank, 24
Weisberg, Danielle, 156
Wheal, Jamie, 94
*White Hot Truth* (LaPorte), 153

## Index

Wilde, Stuart, 83, 115
Wild Soul Movement, 153
Williams, Florence, 91–92
willpower, 105–6
    decision making and, 113
*Willpower* (Baumeister and Tierney), 113
Winfrey, Oprah, 42–43, 136
wings vs. anchors, people as,
    165–66
*Wired,* 26, 100
Woodward, Kathryn, 184

World Domination Summit, 179
Wright, Colin, 165

Y Combinator, 159
Yelp, 179
yourself, listening to, 14, 35–77, 127
YouTube, 163

Zakin, Carly, 156
Zaman, Reema, 64, 163
Zuckerberg, Mark, 91